DRY HUMPING

DRY HUMPING

A Guide to Dating, Relating, and Hooking Up Without the Booze

TAWNY LARA
THE SOBER SEXPERT

QUIRK BOOKS
PHILADELPHIA

Library of Congress Cataloging-in-Publication Data
Names: Lara, Tawny, author.
Title: Dry humping : a guide to dating, relating, and hooking up without the booze / Tawny Lara.
Description: Philadelphia : Quirk Books, [2023] | Includes bibliographical references. | Summary: "A guide to dating, sex, and relationships for people who avoid drinking alcohol, including prompts for self-reflection"–Provided by publisher.
Identifiers: LCCN 2023004815 (print) | LCCN 2023004816 (ebook) | ISBN 9781683693635 (paperback) | ISBN 9781683693642 (ebook)
Subjects: LCSH: Dating (Social customs) | Sex. | Recovering alcoholics.
Classification: LCC HQ801 .L29837 2023 (print) | LCC HQ801 (ebook) | DDC 646.7/7– dc23/eng/20230206
LC record available at https://lccn.loc.gov/2023004815
LC ebook record available at https://lccn.loc.gov/2023004816

ISBN: 978-1-68369-363-5

Printed in China

Typeset in Greycliff, TT Commons, VTC Carrie, Roc Grotesk, Zapf Dingbats, and Sigella

Designed by Paige Graff
Cover photos by Bubball and Prostock-Studio/iStock
Production management by John J. McGurk

Quirk Books
215 Church Street
Philadelphia, PA 19106
quirkbooks.com

10 9 8 7 6 5 4 3 2 1

For Nick, my Sour Humanoid

CONTENTS

Introduction

LETTING GO OF LIQUID COURAGE

In my late twenties, my years of binge drinking, hangovers, and regrettable sex started to take a toll on my overall well-being and love life. I knew that, on some level, I'd have to stop to reevaluate my relationship with alcohol. While I could handle a dry month here and there, one question held me back from ditching the booze for good:

How will I date, let alone have sex, without liquid courage?

Perhaps you, too, have relied on liquid courage to get through a first date or to ask your partner to try something new in bed. Dating, sex, and romance can be scary, and when we're scared, a lot of us outsource our bravery to booze. If you're reading this book, you're probably thinking about drinking less, and like me, you're worried about how you'll handle the anxieties surrounding sex and dating. (I quit drinking altogether, because that's what I needed, but you don't need to commit to complete abstinence to change the way alcohol operates in your love life.)

For starters, you may never have seen a model for healthy, booze-free dating. When it comes to dating and falling in love, many of us learn the ins and outs from movies and TV. Those ins and outs often involve a drink. Tune in to nearly any show or movie to see alcohol depicted as a magical elixir that helps take the edge off whatever might be worrying the characters. The 2018 remake of the film *A Star Is Born* shows Lady Gaga's character taking a shot of tequila before performing her vulnerable love song, "Always Remember Us This Way," for the first time on stage. In the *Big Bang Theory* TV series, Raj morphs from feeling shy around women into feeling overly confident after just one drink. Even Carrie Bradshaw from the iconic TV show *Sex and the City* hypes herself up for an uncomfortable sex talk with her boyfriend with "two-for-the-price-of-one margaritas." I couldn't help but wonder: if Carrie Bradshaw—America's go-to for sex positivity before that term even entered our lexicon—needs alcohol to talk about sex, how do regular people find the courage to engage in uncomfortable or scary dating moments?

Despite what society, Hollywood, and peer pressure might tell you (and what you may say to yourself), you don't need margaritas to navigate the world of dating, sex, and romantic relationships. You just need to learn how to embrace your real, intrinsic courage, which you can access—with a little practice—without booze.

If you've seen Disney's *Dumbo*, remember when the crows give Dumbo (the adorable, floppy-eared elephant) a feather they say is magic, insisting that the feather would make him fly? He later discovered that he could fly all along—the feather wasn't magic, it just gave him the confidence to access the powers he already had. Alcohol may have been a magic feather for you; it may have helped you muster the courage to talk to the cute person at the bar or given you the confidence to have a difficult conversation with a partner. But that's not the same as saying you *need* it. Your desires and abilities were there all along; alcohol just made it easier (maybe sometimes too easy) to ignore your doubts, hesitations, or inhibitions.

What Is Liquid Courage?

The term *liquid courage* dates back to the seventeenth century, when soldiers in the Anglo-Dutch War of 1652 to 1674 drank gin for its biphasic (two-phased) effects. The gin would first calm their nerves, then provide them with a shot of bravery before the battle. We now use the term *liquid courage* colloquially to describe the confidence you might feel after having a few drinks. The battlefield you need to face may be a dimly lit bar or a dating app, but the idea is the same: your shot of bravery is a shortcut to get you ready to deal with something difficult.

But the boldness you get from alcohol is a fleeting feeling that often comes with a side of regret or embarrassment. And while it might be easier to outsource that courage to alcohol, taking the easy route means you never have to get in touch with your inherent bravery.

Because you do have inherent bravery to draw on. If you're cutting back on or quitting alcohol, or even seriously considering it, you are brave! Whether you're coming to terms with a long-term problem and forging a path to recovery, or just reconsidering when and how you use alcohol, passing up booze in a "rosé all day!" culture takes courage. You drew on this courage when you decided to evaluate your relationship with alcohol, and every time you politely decline your family's holiday cocktail or order orange juice in a champagne glass while your friends order bottomless mimosas, it gets stronger. This book helps you bring that intrinsic courage into your love life. The courage to resist relying on alcohol, something we're encouraged to use as a quick fix, means that you can find other ways to take the edge off your anxieties about dating, sex, and romance—from those first date jitters to the anxiety of your first booze-free hookup to the stress of planning a wedding or moving in together.

About Me

I'm not a mental health professional, a doctor, a sexologist, or an official sex expert. So why should you read what I say about sex, dating, and relationships?

I'm a bisexual woman in recovery from substance use disorder and alcohol use disorder who has documented my sobriety journey online since I stopped drinking on November 30, 2015. Before I quit drinking, I lived a stereotypical party girl life in the South. I lived in Waco, Texas, post–Branch Davidians, pre–*Fixer Upper*, mid–NCAA championship run for Baylor's women's basketball team (this is the only sports talk you'll get in this book because it's the only sports talk I know). I bartended from age nineteen to twenty-eight, experiencing the oh-so-boozy restaurant and college bar scene. I spent nearly a decade chugging whiskey in dark bars while wearing a bright smile to mask the pain I barely understood. Working in this environment introduced me to other folks in the same industry. And we partied. Hard.

Managing my drinking felt like a full-time job. So did spending my mornings piecing together the night before, combing through drunk texts and online bank statements and assessing whether I needed to apologize to someone or buy yet another morning-after pill. So I gave up alcohol altogether. I don't know that I'll be sober forever; the thought of never drinking again stresses me out, to be honest.

But I know I'm not going to drink today, and I probably won't drink tomorrow.

I quit on my own, without an official program, shortly after moving to New York City, but you'll hear some jargon used by Alcoholics Anonymous and other twelve-step programs throughout this book because, until the last few years, that's the only language the recovery community had. My DIY recovery program is a syncretic blend of therapy, yoga, writing, and the robust online sober community. I don't come from the AA or twelve-step world, but their "one day at a time" slogan is a valuable mantra that I apply to many facets of life. My goal is to help you take life one *date* at a time, too.

I love to grab a proverbial megaphone to discuss the benefits of living a booze-free life, focusing on the message instead of the mess. I also acknowledge that alcohol served its place in my life. My heavy drinking years actually helped me get through a traumatic time. And let's be honest: I had a damn good time getting wasted. I'm still friends with some of the people I used to party with. We text each other throwback photos from nights of debauchery, laughing at how young and dumb we were. But for every night spent dancing on the bar while shouting "wooo!" to Ke$ha blasting from the speakers, there were countless nights of loneliness, abusive relationships, depression, anxiety, and PTSD. Those dark nights didn't look so glamorous in the light of day—especially when all that repressed depression, anxiety, and PTSD popped up in my sexual or romantic relationships.

I began my journey by connecting with other sober people through blogging, social media, and private Facebook groups. They provided support that helped me grow as a person while learning about why I drank heavily. The online sober space helped me realize that many other people who were sober or sober curious (that is, reevaluating their relationships with alcohol) also struggled with this whole booze-free dating conundrum. There were very few resources about sober intimacy then, and even fewer people were talking about it publicly.

In 2016, before sobriety and dry months became trendy, I searched for answers to my countless questions about sober sex, dating, and relationships in articles, books, podcasts, and other forms of media. I was shocked to discover the lack of resources other than the standard AA advice to "just wait a year."

So I started talking about sober sex and dating on social media. I quickly realized I wasn't the only person who craved these nuanced conversations. I openly discussed my anxieties related to sober sex and dating. Eventually, once I learned how to embrace my authentic courage instead of liquid courage, I realized that booze-free sex and dating were kind of awesome.

Those early Instagram posts evolved from anxious rants about WTF I should do to preaching the gospel of what I learned through personal experience, nerding out over research on how alcohol hinders our sexual experiences, and chatting with sober and sober curious friends about the benefits of alcohol-free sex. I shared how sobriety helped me embrace my bisexuality, how alcohol impairs genital response when society tells us that alcohol amplifies it, how gay bars can often be detrimental to the sexual confidence of queer folks, and so much more that I'll share with you throughout this book.

Then people started directly messaging me with questions about sober sex and dating. I was booked to speak on panels about these topics and commissioned to write articles on them.

Who knew that giving up booze and blogging about it would become the impetus for finding my voice as a writer, falling in love with a sober partner, and becoming the internet's Sober Sexpert? It all started with knowing that I deserved better—and that I had enough real courage, all on my own, to see it through.

Other People You'll Meet in This Book

I want to acknowledge the privilege that comes with my sobriety. I have resources (an understanding family, financial security, health care that provides affordable weekly therapy, and a peer support group that aligns with my values). Many folks can benefit from a booze-free or booze-light life but don't have the means, resources, or support. My ability to become and remain sober also allowed me to step back and then witness and reflect on how alcohol hindered my love life, another privilege that I know many people don't have. That's why this book is written with the insight of my fellow sober and sober curious peers.

This book acknowledges that the booze-free dating scene for a corporate executive making six figures who attends AA meetings might be different from the booze-free dating scene for a single parent juggling multiple minimum wage jobs who attends online peer support groups while cooking dinner.

The personal stories I share here are anecdotes from a white-passing, cisgender woman of Mexican and Jewish descent. My experiences don't speak for the sober or sober curious community. So, in addition to interviewing licensed, trained, and qualified mental health professionals and sexual health professionals, I've also interviewed folks with different life experiences. You'll also see me use terms like *sober, in recovery, booze-free, alcohol-free,* and *sober curious* so this book is as inclusive as possible of different relationships with alcohol and sobriety.

SAY WHAT? SOBER CURIOUS

Someone who's curious about evaluating their relationship with alcohol. Maybe they'll drink occasionally. Perhaps they'll stop drinking altogether. Ruby Warrington, the author of the book *Sober Curious* and host of the podcast of the same name, coined this term in 2015.

I don't mean to be flippant when I say that people in long-term recovery and those who participate in the occasional dry month are on the same path. I'm aware that these are two very different life journeys. But the longer I write about alcohol-free sex and dating, the more I notice that the advice is the same whether someone's been sober for decades or is just interested in recalibrating their relationship with alcohol. Adversity is a universal experience; we're all recovering from something.

In this book, you'll meet folks across the gender spectrum (trans, cis, and nonbinary) and the sexuality spectrum (straight, gay, pansexual/bisexual, asexual). Some people I talked to are neurodivergent (ADHD, dyslexic), and some have physical disabilities. You'll also meet people from different ethnic backgrounds and different socioeconomic statuses: customer service workers, wealthy one-percenters, sex workers, doctors, and students.

Regarding relationship diversity, I interviewed single folks, people in long-term or married relationships, parents, polyamorous partners, and people with zero interest in sex or romance. These fantastic humans offer nuanced insight into the world of alcohol use and share how they learned to go on a damn date without booze. Everyone I spoke to shares a common desire to reevaluate their relationships with alcohol and how that desire intersects with their love lives.

I also want to be clear that I'm not anti-alcohol. I'm aware that many people can have a beer or three without those drinks having negative consequences in their lives. Giving up alcohol helped me find the best version of myself, which helped me create a healthier love life. My goal is for you to be mindful of how alcohol intersects (or doesn't!) with your romantic and sexual self.

This book is for you regardless of where you are on your booze-free journey. It's the guide that newly sober me so desperately needed. This book is hyperfocused on the sex, dating, and relationship aspect of booze-free life. It's not an official lesson on how to get sober, but I'll cite resources and quote many wonderful authors who write about sobriety throughout the text. I wrote this guide with the full spectrum of booze-free folks in mind. Twenty years sober? You're in the right place. Considering a dry month? Hell yeah, you're also in the right place. Done with alcohol but still love cannabis and psychedelics? You can totally sit with us!

So buckle up. Grab a fizzy kombucha. And let's dry hump.

You're Definitely Not Alone

Worried you'll look like a weirdo for not drinking on a date? Let's be real: you're the normal one here! Not only are more and more people reevaluating their relationship with alcohol, but there have always been lots of people who don't drink for various reasons, such as the following.

- Religion and philosophy: Some belief systems forbid or discourage the use of alcohol and other intoxicants.

- Health conditions: Alcohol affects certain medical conditions. Drinking can also interact negatively with medications, herbal supplements, or vitamins. (And yes, sometimes people are pregnant!)

- Wellness and fitness: Lots of people in the fitness community eschew alcohol altogether or practice mindful drinking while training.

- Low-sugar dietary restrictions: Alcohol has a high proportion of sugar (often a lot!) to nutritional value (basically none), meaning that people with diabetes or anyone on a low-sugar diet might opt to go without.

- Work: People whose jobs require mental acuity and decision-making on short notice, such as paramedics, may choose not to drink when on call or ever.

- Preference: Some people just don't like alcohol. I know, this one throws me off, too!

PART 1

DRY DATING

CHAPTER 1

DATING YOURSELF

It's no secret that the most important relationship in your life is your relationship with yourself. To get in touch with your intrinsic courage or go on a booze-free date or have sober sex, you must reconnect with who you are without alcohol. Dating yourself in this context means getting to know your interests, passions, and turn-ons, even if you're already in a relationship. This reconnection might look like replacing boozy brunch with a weekend writing class, or it might mean something a little less tangible—like unlearning some of the societal tropes that convince us that we're weird for ditching booze or drinking less. I know this all sounds heavy, but I'm here to hold your hand as we take this ride together!

Taking the time to date yourself without alcohol can help you show up more authentically confidently on dates or in your existing relationship. It lets you get in touch with your intrinsic courage in a low-pressure way, so you know what it feels like when you need to access that courage for scarier scenarios.

I stumbled upon the importance of dating myself by accident. I wasn't ready to do the emotional work of figuring out how to go on a date without alcohol, so I procrastinated by volunteering, reading quit lit, and training for a half-marathon. When I felt emotionally ready to peel back some layers, I started with myself mostly because I couldn't think of where else to start. But as it turns out, this period of reflecting and getting to know my sober self was the best strategy I could have envisioned. A significant part of dating myself was (and still is) working through my body image issues, which had led me to alcohol as a shortcut to feeling confident on dates and during sex. That alone time in early sobriety allowed me to meet and embrace the real me, the version I often drank to avoid.

SAY WHAT? QUIT LIT

Literature about **quit**ting drinking (or other substances). The term is primarily used to mean memoirs or self-help books about sobriety. Check out the QuitLit hashtag on social media to learn more about these books!

But dating yourself isn't just about self-knowledge or introspection. Dates would be boring if we *only* sat there learning about each other (or ourselves, in this case). When you're in the self-dating period of resetting your relationship with alcohol, you should literally take yourself out on some dates! If grabbing a drink after work is your go-to, try replacing that with a new ritual—maybe you take a spin through the bookstore after work instead. Take yourself to the movies, to a restaurant, or to a mocktail mixology class to practice getting out there without getting drunk. My (also sober) partner, Nick, jokes that he liked taking himself out to dinner when he was single because he knew he'd always enjoy the company and always put out at the end of the night.

The first step in replacing liquid courage with actual courage begins in the mirror. When we remove alcohol from our lives, even temporarily, we're left with the natural, unfiltered version of ourselves.

BODY IMAGE BEYOND BOOZE

Like many people, I have body image issues that stem from childhood teasing and the pressures that society places on women. In kindergarten, I had warts on my arms and legs, so kids called me Rice Krispie Girl. I wore long-sleeve shirts year-round, hiding my arms until I got the warts burned off. In middle school, kids called me Toucan Sam because my nose was "too big," so I obsessed over classmates with what I saw as perfect noses, hoping to get a nose job one day. (I never did.) My first long-term relationship was with a man who called me Spike: a portmanteau of "spic," a derogatory word for someone of Latin heritage, and "kike," a derogatory term for a Jewish person. In my early twenties, someone asked me if I was pregnant after I put on ten pounds. These unnecessary, hurtful judgments built upon one another, then mixed with society's eternal projection of the ideal woman, leading to me develop body dysmorphic disorder (BDD).

BDD is a mental health condition in which you obsess over specific aspects of your face or body. These supposed flaws seem unremarkable to other people, but your belief that they are deformed or grotesque affects your self-image and your ability to function socially. For me, I frequently see a distorted version of myself in the mirror and hyperfixate on my stomach. Many people whose BDD centers on their weight or body size develop eating disorders, but it's also common for folks with BDD to outsource their confidence to liquid courage. I fell into the latter group, using alcohol to feel more confident about my self-determined problem areas during sex. A 2017 study in the *Journal of Obsessive-Compulsive and Related Disorders* examines the alcohol use of 101 people with diagnosed BDD. An unsurprising 49.5 percent reported drinking when feeling insecure about their bodies, and 59.4 percent said drinking alcohol helped them feel more confident in their appearance.

This outsourcing does a disservice to our psyche, as it continuously reinforces the idea that alcohol is a viable shortcut to confidence. Not only are you missing out on countless ways to build self-confidence, but you're also hindering your ability to grow. You grow by doing challenging things, not by being drunk or buzzed to get through the tough stuff. As Amanda White, a millennial therapist with a huge social media following (you may have seen her viral videos on topics like boundary setting) and the author of *Not Drinking Tonight: A Guide to Creating a Sober Life You Love*, put it to me, "Confidence comes from knowing things are hard and doing them anyway. Then you feel better, and then you can do it again."

When I share my tales of BDD with others, they all have their own version—regardless of gender. My woes about my "imperfect stomach" are usually met with cries of "well, at least your [*insert least favorite body part*] isn't [*insert hateful thing that you'd never say even to an enemy*]." Self-hatred appears to be a language we all speak fluently. So it makes sense that we collectively search for a solution in the form of liquid courage to give us just a few moments of fleeting body confidence in the bedroom.

I polled some of my Instagram followers, asking a range of questions that focus on the intersection of body image and alcohol use disorder (AUD). Of the 76 people who participated, 71 percent said alcohol made them feel more confident with their bodies. Two-thirds admitted to drinking alcohol to cope with their body image, and 85 percent shared that they felt more confident in their bodies while flirting after having a few drinks. While these poll results validated some of my lingering body insecurities, I wanted to dig a little deeper, so I phoned a friend.

I spoke with Aqxyl Storms, an alcohol-free nonbinary musician, about how some people turn to alcohol to ease general anxiety about their physical presentation. "I think my eating disorder had a lot to do with the discomfort I felt in my physical body. I liked to drink because it made me feel way less awkward," they shared. Aqxyl's sober curiosity began with a dry month in the early days of the COVID-19 pandemic and even resulted in them opening Minus Moonshine, a booze-free bottle shop in Crown Heights, Brooklyn. "Giving up alcohol helped me learn to accept my weirdness and awkwardness, not just with my body but also my personality," they told me. "My confidence is real for the first time in my adulthood. I've also met a lot of other socially anxious people through the shop. It's great to be myself with nonjudgmental people, no alcohol needed."

Being able to face your body with real courage, not just liquid courage, can mean gaining the space to make changes that will let you feel better for good—not just in the moment. Dubbs Weinblatt, a transgender educator and the host of the *Thank You for Coming Out* podcast, began gender-affirming hormone therapy just one month and six days after they stopped drinking during the COVID-19 pandemic. "I started out doing a dry month. I just wanted a reset," they said during a Zoom interview. Before that dry month, Weinblatt's only other experience with temporary sobriety in twenty years was the two weeks before their top surgery. "As soon as I stopped drinking, it opened up the headspace for me to try T [testosterone] sooner," Weinblatt told me. "I take my shot of T every Monday. Those moments are full of gender euphoria. When I was drinking, I was just going through the motions of survival mode." Weinblatt hasn't had a drink since June 1, 2020!

Paulina Pinsky, a sober writer who openly discusses their history with eating disorders and body confidence, also found that when they stopped outsourcing their body image to alcohol, they were able to take real steps to repair their relationship with their body. "Alcohol instilled false confidence," they told me in an email. "It made it easier to talk to people—to say things I wanted to say sober but felt too afraid to admit. Now I know that I can say what I'm thinking, and I make it a priority to do so—even if it is difficult. I am so much more than a pair of tits and ass. But nowadays, I am much more concerned about putting together a killer outfit than looking any particular way. My body is my own, and isn't that a gift?" Looking at your body as your own can be incredibly powerful, especially if you've experienced sexual trauma. (We'll go deeper into the intersection of alcohol and sexual trauma in a later chapter.)

Alcohol turned off my self-consciousness switch, helping me feel flirtier with people I was attracted to and be more direct when asking for what I wanted. Those perceived physical flaws that I obsessed over didn't seem as crucial when I was inebriated. I had no idea that my self-confidence was intertwined with alcohol's empty promise of liquid courage until I stopped drinking. I had to find other ways to feel confident in my body without using alcohol as a prop.

And like Weinblatt and Pinsky, I found that accessing this inner confidence helped me fix the real issue—which wasn't my body at all, but the way I spoke about it and let other people speak about it. As my friend Ginny Hogan, a comedian who gave up alcohol in March 2019, explained to me, the confidence you find in the absence of booze also helps you avoid situations that undermine your self-love in the future. "Alcohol helped me feel more confident in my body for sure," she shared in an email exchange. "I can't say that I've gotten as comfortable sober, but one huge pro is now I don't sleep with someone who doesn't make me feel confident in my body." Her last sentiment resonates deeply with me. I often settled for any form of sexual attention, even negative, when I drank. "Because I don't have booze around, I have higher standards," Ginny continues. Me too, girl!

Why You Should Date Yourself (Even If You're Partnered Up!)

Prioritizing sobriety or sober curiosity goes hand in hand with putting your mental health first. Something in you knew that you needed to reevaluate your relationship with alcohol. Then you took it a step further to explore how drinking intersects with your love life. But before you can show up for others in a sexual or romantic way, you must take care of yourself first.

Here are a few reasons why dating yourself is an essential part of the dry dating journey:

- It's a chance to learn which topics genuinely interest you without the external influence of alcohol or someone else's input. Sharing these newfound interests on a date then helps your possible new partner get to know you on a deeper level.

- Exploring your body solo can help you discover new turn-ons. It can also help you figure out what you don't like. Knowing your turn-ons and turn-offs can make partnered sex even better!

- Quality alone time allows you to reflect on your booze-free journey through therapy or journaling. Processing these important life moments can give you language and perspective that can help you share those feelings with a partner.

HOW TO FEEL CONFIDENT WITHOUT BOOZE

If you've been outsourcing your body confidence to liquid courage, you're not alone. One of the most common questions I receive through Instagram and email is, "How do I feel secure with a date or in the bedroom without having a drink first?" Instead of relying on the fleeting bravado alcohol may provide, let's discuss tools to boost your self-esteem that won't leave you with a hangover.

Explore New Hobbies

In his early sobriety, my partner (although he wasn't my partner at the time), Nick, read an article about how to make vinegar, so he gave it a shot. "As a sommelier, I got lots of free wine. Making vinegar gave me a creative way to use the wine I wasn't drinking anymore," he shared. It turns out he's pretty good at fermentation. That hobby, paired with his sommelier skills, led him to launch an artisanal vinegar line (it's called Sour Humanoid if you want to look it up) and meet new people he wouldn't have met otherwise. Nick's sobriety gave him the space to explore creative ideas which helped him grow into a charming person with a personality outside of booze.

Nurturing his creative side also gave him something to talk about with dates. He texted me photos of his kitchen cabinet filled with different types of vinegars-in-progress a few days after we met. To some people, those mason jars filled with slime and bacteria might be weird, but I found it endearing that he wanted to share his hobby with me—a hobby that he might never have explored if he kept pouring the wine into his belly instead of fermenting it into something else.

Take Some Classes

Early sobriety left me with lots of extra time and money, but I want to acknowledge that others often have the polar opposite experience. Many people go to rehab, detox centers, or other treatment programs that cost vast amounts of money and aren't always covered by insurance (and that's if you're not one of the 31.6 million Americans who are uninsured). In my case, though, giving up booze *saved* me money. I finally had a surplus of time and extra cash on hand that I was no longer spending on alcohol, so I put both toward enrichment courses. I had always told myself that I'd learn Spanish *one day* or take that writing class *sometime*. Sobriety let me make those hypothetical to-do lists happen for real.

My mom joked that I created a DIY master's degree because I took so many classes. I studied Spanish, working through levels as my español improved. I took memoir writing classes, workshopping some essays and book ideas with peers. I even tried out comedy courses. I studied improv (cringe!) and sketch comedy writing because I wanted to learn how to talk about mental health and alcohol abuse with a sense of humor. The common thread in these courses is that I met future dates and new friends. It didn't matter if they drank or not because we shared an interest greater than sitting at the bar.

Try a Mirror Exercise

In early sobriety, I wrote a sex column for an Australian website. Most assignments entailed such things as interviewing dominatrices, researching how to sell worn panties online for quick cash, and of course, reviewing sex toys. My edgiest assignment was to masturbate in front of a mirror and then write about it. I didn't think twice; I'm usually down to try new things—especially if I'm paid. I was a sex columnist, after all.

Much of my boozy sex life (even my solo sex life) had performative elements. I had an idea of what I was supposed to look like when turned on. *My stomach should have no rolls when I move my body. I must look flawless at any given moment. My face should look ladylike while climaxing.* I modeled this curated version of myself after the porn I grew up watching before I knew about the magic of studio video editing, flattering angles, and intentional lighting and before I realized that porn was its own form of acting. This was also before I worked through my sexual trauma with a therapist and realized that porn is entertainment, not a how-to manual.

I initially approached my mirror assignment as a chance to check whether my body looked good enough to do such a courageous act in front of someone else. I wanted to see, the way someone else would see, how my face looked while aroused. What my vulva looked like when stimulated. How my body twitched and reacted to being touched in sensitive places. But as I did the exercise, it became instead a way to challenge my sex-related insecurities and learn to prioritize my own pleasure, regardless of how it might look to someone else.

In all its cringeworthy glory, that mirror exercise helped me connect with my body as it was, rather than worrying about what others thought of it. I laughed at the awkwardness of seeing all of me moving in ways I'd never seen my body move before. I accepted that I don't look like the actors and porn stars I tried to emulate—because they're performing in a studio, and even *they* don't look like their on-screen characters—and embraced the person I am.

This exercise reminded me that I'm a human who deserves love and pleasure—regardless of how I look in the mirror. I chatted about it with another sober internet friend, Bethany Stevens, a PhD student of sociology, disability scholar, and sexologist. "Mirror exercises are great for anyone, but even more so for people who've experienced sexual trauma," she said. "Empowering yourself to know that you get to own your body is a big step. It's useful to know that you can generate your own pleasure, and it's not somebody else's." This literal reflection period connected me with the intrinsic courage I later brought into my dating life.

Spend one-on-one time with your mirror while getting ready for a sober date. OK, you don't have to do *that* mirror exercise, but if you're already looking in the mirror on your way out the door, why not try this quick exercise: say (out loud!) what you like about the person looking back at you. Maybe your hair looks awesome, or you feel good about nailing a presentation at work earlier in the week. Verbally celebrating those wins before you leave your house might leave you feeling confident about that date. That's the intrinsic courage I'm talking about!

Move Your Body

Countless studies prove the link between exercise and neurotransmitters like dopamine and endorphins. You know that runner's high people talk about? That's the endorphins talking. For years I thought of exercise as something people only did to lose weight. I didn't understand why skinny people worked out. Now I get it: movement quite literally makes us feel good. I talked to Amber van de Bunt, a.k.a. Karmen Karma, an adult performer and the author of *Overcome: A Memoir of Abuse, Addiction, Sex Work, and Recovery*, about the benefit of incorporating endorphins into your booze-free journey. "I got sober by replacing the addiction," she told me. "I got natural endorphins from the gym, which gave me a healthy outlet to put my energy into." The idea behind replacing addictions works just like van de Bunt said: finding a healthy way to channel that same energy. If incorporating exercise triggers dangerous behaviors, then that's a sign of an *un*healthy outlet. Getting your endorphin fix has all kinds of beneficial results, for your mind as well as your body. Establishing healthy habits and a steady routine gave me a sense of accomplishment, organically boosting my confidence.

You don't have to run a marathon or join a gym to stimulate these neurotransmitters. The important thing here is movement. Movement can look like going for a walk, playing with your kids in the backyard, or taking yourself dancing. Remember: you're dating yourself right now!

Though I got into yoga during my drinking days, my yoga practice grew deeper once I gave up booze. Having a form of exercise that challenges my body and mind provides tangible body goals that aren't tied to weight loss. I no longer strive to see a certain number on the scale. Instead, I celebrate when my body can move deeper into a pose than it could two months before. I also give myself grace when my body can't do something today that it could do last week. This authentic confidence and grace also shows up off the mat. These humbling moments remind me that I can still have a little fun when a date doesn't go the way I thought it would.

Achieve Some Realistic Goals

Sure, sex is great, but have you ever completed a to-do list? The feeling of accomplishment that comes from crossing items off my to-do list inspires me to keep that momentum going. Creating, then achieving some approachable goals can provide lasting, positive effects for your self-esteem. I'm not talking about those masochistic New Year's resolution–style goals, like giving up sugar or working out for an hour a day. I'm talking about doing more tangible esteem-able acts and then celebrating those wins. These acts can be anything from offering to babysit for a friend who needs some alone time to volunteering for a nonprofit that aligns with your values, sending a handwritten thank-you note to someone you love, or even paying that bill you're ignoring.

SAY WHAT? ESTEEMABLE ACTS

According to lawyer and motivational speaker Francine Ward, who has written about the role of these actions in her addiction recovery, esteemable acts are small, daily behaviors that contribute to self-esteem.

Amanda White, the millennial therapist, talked to me about how setting goals in early sobriety or sober curiosity can organically build confidence. "There's a very specific erosion of self-esteem that happens if you're constantly breaking promises to yourself," she told me. "When you're in the habit of saying things to yourself and then breaking all these promises, you don't learn to trust yourself or your word. It's important in early sobriety or sober curiosity that people are careful with the promises they're making to themselves. Start with small goals and slowly build confidence over time." Crossing those tasks off your to-do list can help you learn to trust yourself.

Dating yourself—taking yourself out, exploring new things, getting comfortable with your body, building trust with yourself, and spending time really getting to know the person you are—is a necessary first step in learning to access real confidence and real courage without the booze. Now that you're fully crushing on yourself, we can talk about flirting with other people, too!

CHAPTER 2

GETTING OUT THERE

Our lives, friend groups, and confidence are often so tied to alcohol that we forget what dating was like before reaching an age where everyone started meeting for drinks.

Comedian Nick Kroll's show *Human Resources*, a spin-off of Netflix's coming-of-age cartoon comedy *Big Mouth*, appropriately features a bar named The Mistake Factory. This is the local watering hole where the characters get wasted and then make bad decisions. That name makes me laugh, but it also really resonates with me—I've had my fair share of booze-induced mistakes. If you're reading this book, you probably have, too. While there are plenty of people who met in bars and then fell in love and lived happily ever after (whatever that means), there are just as many people who cringe when they think about that one person (or those many people) they dated or hooked up with while wasted.

Before I got sober, all my relationships and hookups began in my hometown's various Mistake Factories. A dark room filled with liquidly courageous people donning beer goggles sounds like an easy place to meet someone. You're already loose from a drink or two, so why not chat up a stranger? You barely have to worry about impressing them, since you're both drunk! Sure, you have to shout over the pulsing beats of today's hottest song to hear each other, but those external distractions can also distract us from ourselves.

But for me, and I'd guess for a lot of folks, it never worked out long-term with the people I met in bars. Maybe because we were both stuck, unaware of how to take the next step in our lives, let alone merge paths with someone else. Or maybe it's because we didn't have much in common other than our shared affinity for drink specials and the uninhibited sex that frequently followed. But even though I kept striking out, I never thought to look for a mate outside of a bar until I quit drinking.

Meeting people in places other than a bar may feel intimidating or uncomfortable at first because it's scary to do things alone without alcohol to take the edge off your anxiety. The following tips can help you to tap into your intrinsic courage.

CONNECTING WITH WHY YOU'RE DATING WITHOUT ALCOHOL

Before you go on a date, before you have sober sex for the first time, before you talk to your partner or partners about your booze-free plans, you must figure out *why* you're stepping back to evaluate the role that alcohol plays in your love life. You may get some pushback from future dates, current partners, and even your friends and family who just don't understand why you're trying to drink less or not drink at all. When faced with these uncomfortable moments, it can help to keep a sentence or two in your back pocket for a quick reply. Here are a few ways to access that "why":

- ❤ Write down why you usually (or used to) drink on dates. What did alcohol bring to the experience? What did it take away? Read what you just wrote to notice any themes or standout lines. You can turn this into your mantra or personalized affirmation.

- ❤ Ask a friend to text you this mantra when you're out on a date, or at random times, as a simple reminder of why you're choosing to date alcohol-free right now. Or better yet, schedule these affirmations as emails to yourself.

- ❤ Plug these sentences into a photo app to create a DIY lock screen or backdrop for your phone.

- ❤ Write your why on sticky notes and place them around your home.

These self-generated affirmations may come in handy when you feel like throwing in the towel on sober dating.

Benefits of Dry Dating

Maybe liquid courage helps you feel more social on a date, but at what cost? Removing alcohol from your dating experience can have profoundly positive effects. Getting in touch with your emotions might help you form an organic bond with your date. And while looks don't always matter, I'd be remiss if I didn't mention some of the physical benefits of giving up booze or drinking less. Here's a quick rundown of the perks of dry dating.

EMOTIONAL

- Just one or two drinks can prevent the brain from creating memories. Sober dating lets you remember the conversations you have and the activities you participate in.

- Excessive drinking can lead to poor decision-making and reduced brain function. A clear mind means you're less likely do something (or someone!) you might regret in the morning.

- Showing up with your intrinsic courage instead of liquid courage lets you meet someone as they truly are while presenting who *you* truly are.

- You can reevaluate past relationships so you don't make the same mistakes.

- You have the clarity to evaluate if this is a person you want to spend more time with.

- Removing the beer goggles helps you see red flags that could easily be missed after a few drinks.

PHYSICAL

- Alcohol can dehydrate your skin. So booze-free dating might mean clearer, brighter skin.

- Booze might lead to water retention, so switching to a fun, nonalcoholic drink can reduce hangover-induced bloating.

- Alcohol is known to disrupt your REM cycle. A good night of sleep without a nightcap (or two) might mean no under-eye bags or dark circles.

- No slurred words, bloodshot eyes, or embarrassing drunk texts. Enough said.

FINANCIAL

- Ditching booze on dates is usually cheaper. If you're used to spending a certain amount on drinks, put that money toward an exciting, experiential date.

- Alcohol can make us behave frivolously in many aspects of adulting, especially when it comes to saving (or not saving) money. Cutting back can give you a chance to finally stick to that budget.

- Waking up without a hangover the morning after a night out means brunch might be cheaper too—no pricey hair of the dog!

LOOKING FOR SOBER PARTNERS

Limiting yourself to partners who don't drink won't be the right choice for everyone, but it certainly has some advantages. I had a virtual meeting with sober power couple Austin and Lara Cooper during the early pandemic days. "Before I met Lara, I used dating apps," Austin told me, while smiling at Lara. "I found myself on dates with people who turned out to be hardcore partiers. That didn't work for me because it reminded me of my dark past." Austin and Lara are both outspoken advocates for sobriety, and both post regularly on Instagram about how getting sober improved their lives. Once they finally had the chance to meet in person, a love connection quickly formed. "Sober people are often self-aware and they're usually into bettering themselves. It's also nice to have someone who's been through what you've been through. A sober partner understands it," Lara shared. I relate to this on a personal level since my partner and I met in a way that illustrates this exact idea.

I've already mentioned that AA wasn't my jam, but I did meet my partner there. In the fall of 2018, I was almost three years sober and had a major depressive episode. This episode was triggered by a habitual cycle I repeatedly found myself in: I'd overfill my plate with freelance work and saying yes to too many social obligations, and freak out when I realized I just couldn't do it all. Then I'd shamefully back out of my prior commitments, feeling like a disappointment to myself and the people I canceled on. It was part people-pleasing, part trying to stay busy so I didn't have to feel too much, and part plain ol' anxiety. Overcommitting and bailing on commitments both started as coping mechanisms, but—like drinking—they weren't working anymore.

Once I pulled myself out of bed, I realized I needed more help than weekly therapy and the occasional peer support groups I attended. So I looked up AA meetings in my area, because being in a room with other sober people, even if we don't agree on the twelve steps, helps me get out of my head. The meeting's topic was romantic entanglements and how dating someone from your support group can get messy. And, of course, that's the moment that Nick and I locked eyes. I noticed he was wearing a Bob Dylan shirt, so I had found my in. I patiently waited for my opportunity to drop an offhand "I like your shirt," finally managing to do it after the group serenity prayer. "I like *your* shirt," he replied. I had on a crop top emblazoned with a lion mid-roar. It turned out he had also been waiting for the perfect moment to say, "I like your shirt." We still joke about this today when we wear those shirts!

Our first dates were atypical. They were daily activities that we'd do alone anyway, like walking his dog or attending a support group. It felt comfortable and loving from day one. There were no "Should I text?" or "Is it OK to say this?" games. It helped that we had already done a lot of work on ourselves, in our own sobriety, before we tried to be true partners to someone else. The bond that Nick and I have isn't just because we don't drink; it's because not drinking taught us how to communicate. "AA taught me how to talk about my feelings. Something society doesn't usually teach men is accessible in peer support groups," he shared with me.

Meeting in a support group worked for Nick and me, but meeting people this way can also lead to trauma bonding, where a relationship is formed based on a shared traumatic experience. Nick and I each had three years of sobriety before we met in that room. This is significantly different than two people meeting in rehab, or someone with multiple years of sobriety hitting on a newcomer (the latter is often called thirteenth stepping).

> ## SAY WHAT? TRAUMA BOND
>
> An intense emotional attachment born of trauma or abuse, either to the person perpetrating the abuse or to someone else with a shared experience of trauma.

If you do connect with someone in a support group, rehab, or other vulnerable spot, therapist Lynn Macarin-Mara (in fact, my amazing therapist!) has a few questions for you to ask yourself to avoid forming a trauma bond:

- ❤ Is this the type of person I am usually attracted to?
- ❤ Am I looking at this person realistically, taking note of where they are in their life?
- ❤ Am I ignoring some negative relationship behaviors?
- ❤ Am I beginning to feel anxious in this relationship?
- ❤ Do they follow through with things?
- ❤ How are they when it comes to intimacy?
- ❤ What kind of social support do they have?
- ❤ What kind of relationships do they have with their family?
- ❤ Are they similar to the kind of person you've been drawn to before?

Being Queer Outside the Bar

Queer folks may have an especially difficult time finding places to meet that don't center on alcohol, due to the significance of gay bars in queer culture. For many of us, it was a rite of passage: turn eighteen, then go to the gay bar. It's the one safe space where we can be with *our people*, away from family disappointment or peer bullying. But that haven comes with a cost of its own.

The gay bar gives us a break from societal expectations of cisgender, heterosexual attraction, but it keeps the expectation of drinking—and when the bar is one of your only options for dating or socializing, that pressure looms large. "A nightclub is the first place that a lot of folks who are queer receive positive attention for their sexuality and self-expression for their body," Mike Rosen, MS Ed., a psychotherapist and public speaker, told me. "If the gay bar is the first place where you feel like you're able to express yourself, then it makes sense that you would think it's the main place or possibly even the only place. A healthier way to look at the gay bar might be, 'If I can be accepted here, where else might I be accepted? Where are all these people during the day?'"

But queer people get sober too, and a rising trend to create alcohol-free havens for queer folks is popping up nationwide. "Gay bars have long been a staple of queer communing, organizing, protesting, and of course hooking up, but alcohol-focused environments aren't ideal for a sizable facet of a community that also faces increased risk of addiction and substance abuse issues," Trish Bendix writes in her 2019 *Them* article titled "Sober Queer Spaces Are Giving LGBTQ+ People a Place to Just Be." Check local listings—you're likely to find a queer bookstore, coffee shop, museum, or booze-free meetup in your area.

COMING OUT AS BOOZE-FREE

If you don't organically connect with someone in an alcohol-free space, the question that might hang over your head is, "When do I tell them I don't drink?" I refer to this topic as coming out as booze-free—this is a little tongue-in-cheek, since it's not as fraught as coming out as queer and much less likely to lead to negative consequences, but I want to acknowledge that in the moment it can *feel* like a truly momentous conversation. And it comes up whether you've been sober for a few years or you're temporarily giving up booze for a month.

There are a few different points in a relationship when you can introduce the topic. They're all a little awkward—this is all awkward because dating is awkward!—but they all have things to recommend them, too. Consider the following options when you're planning your dates, and pick the one that feels right to you.

Put *Booze-Free* on Your Dating Profile

Pro: Openly claiming that you're booze-free, even temporarily, on dating profiles is a bold yet efficient move. Bold because it shows that you're unapologetically proud to be booze-free; efficient because it also shows that you're not interested in wasting your time with folks who may have issues dating someone who's not drinking right now. (Yes, people do swipe left because of this!)

Con: In my personal experience, adding *sober* to my dating profile led to some people only wanting to discuss sobriety. (Read: telling me that they don't drink *that* much or letting me know that their uncle just got out of rehab.) This conversation often led to me acting as their armchair therapist, which felt deeply unsexy. You can look at this convo as a red flag or a helpful screening mechanism.

Gabby Valdes, a dating coach and the host of the *Finally Found You* podcast, recommends this approach for people who are committed to not drinking for at least some amount of time—but she also acknowledges that it likely won't be the right move for people who are still unsure about their relationship with alcohol. "Putting 'booze-free' or 'sober' on your dating profile isn't for everyone, especially folks that may not know exactly how they feel about alcohol or how their relationship with alcohol intersects with sex and dating just yet," she said on our Instagram Live chat about sober sex and dating. "You want your online dating profile to showcase who you are, instead of a polished version" who may be more certain about sobriety than you really are. The goal here is to establish a conscious connection, so honesty is vital.

You can also take a more subtle approach to authenticity, dropping hints for other non-drinkers to pick up on. I've seen some dating app profiles say, "Friend of Bill W.," which is coded, insider lingo referencing the founder of Alcoholics Anonymous. I've also seen folks put "One Day at a Time" or the more enigmatic and modern "ODAAT" in their bios. These code words are specifically AA-focused, but more casual non-drinkers might mention getting "coffee or juice" or throw in a line like "I'd love to meet anywhere but a bar." The idea is to catch the eye of people who are open to non-boozy dating, without having to make a big statement.

Tell Them IRL

Pro: Disclosing your booze-free status to your date(s) in person gives you the chance to feel comfortable with them before sharing something so personal. "The 'sober' talk doesn't have to be a serious conversation," Valdes told me—and it doesn't have to happen right away. "When you're out on a date, simply order a nonalcoholic drink. You can wait until the first (or second or tenth!) date to mention that you don't drink." If your date takes issue with you not drinking, that might be a clear sign that this person isn't right for you.

On the flip side, if they respond well, that can be a welcome green flag. Lisa Smith, author of *Girl Walks Out of a Bar* and my cohost on the *Recovery Rocks* podcast, waited until the fifth date to tell her now-husband that she didn't drink. Like many of us, she had anxiety about sharing something so personal with someone she liked. "I'm sure you've noticed I don't drink alcohol," she told him. His comical response: "You don't? So you'll be a cheap date!" She appreciated that his lighthearted response saw an added value in dating a sober person: saving money on date night!

Con: It could get awkward. You may have to chalk the date up as a waste of time for everyone involved. "Some people don't like surprises or don't want to drink alone," my partner, Nick, said. "One time, I waited until the first date to tell someone I didn't drink, and she felt insecure about drinking a glass of wine while I drank club soda." Dating is already filled with enough insecurities and pitfalls, so you may not want to risk adding more—other options allow you to let people know before the date, so both of you have a chance to call the whole thing off if they don't react well.

Tell Them in a DM, Text, or Phone Call

Pro: Getting vulnerable with a potential date over DM (or some other one-on-one communication outside of a date context) can be a happy medium between options one and two. It's not as in-your-face as putting *sober* or *booze-free* on your profile, but it serves as its own form of efficiency. Private messages and voice memos on dating apps or social media offer a few options to connect before you decide to meet IRL or hop on a FaceTime call. When the time feels right, you can tell them that you're sober or not drinking right now (whatever feels true for you). Their response will let you know how they feel about possibly dating someone who doesn't drink. If they lose interest, you find out before obsessing over an outfit and styling your hair. This approach also allows you to plan a creative booze-free date (see page 54 for ideas) or find a restaurant with nonalcoholic drink options.

Con: DMs are usually a lighthearted way to get to know each other before meeting IRL, and it's hard to predict how potential dates will react to your bringing up something potentially serious. Like mentioning not drinking in your profile, this can sometimes lead to uncomfortable interactions. They may talk *at* you, confiding about their relationship with alcohol or using you as an open-door confessional. Then again, if they're going to behave that way, it's probably better to know now!

Try a Booze-Free Dating App or Sober Filter

Pro: The rise in dry dating mixed with our "there's an app for that" culture means that there are now several dating apps specifically for those who don't imbibe. The popularity of these apps pushed some of the more well-known dating apps to implement a sober filter. Search your app store for "sober dating," then download a few options to give them a try. You and your potential match have something in common right off the bat: not drinking. There's no need to worry about how to bring up the "I don't drink" convo when you meet in a sober environment.

SAY WHAT? DRY DATING

Keeping your dating life free of alcohol, whether or not you're a drinker in other situations.

Con: You may not want to limit yourself to non-drinkers! Not everyone cares whether their dates drink or not, and any filter is going to constrain your options—not to mention the fact that dry dating apps are relatively new and may have fewer users than a more established app. There may not be as many fish swimming in the seltzer sea as there are in the wider waters.

No matter when and how you decide to introduce the topic, clear communication is of the utmost importance if you're telling a date that you're trying to drink less or not at all. Consider emphasizing what sobriety (or temporary sobriety) gives you instead of what you think is missing. For example, "I can't drink right now" becomes "I'm taking a break from hangovers" or "I've been finding that I have way more energy when I don't drink alcohol." Focusing on the positive shows that you're in control and happy about your decision to step away from booze for a bit.

SAMPLE CONVERSATIONS

No matter how carefully you choose your moment and your approach, some folks may not support your decision to give up alcohol, even temporarily. It may not always be clear how the person sitting across the table receives the information you just told them. Are they supportive of your decision not to drink? Are they getting defensive about their drinking habits? Are they asking how they can be supportive? Are they indifferent and excited to order appetizers? Here are some possible responses you might hear.

Defensive

- ❤ "I don't drink *that* often."
- ❤ "I tried the whole sobriety thing once. It wasn't for me."
- ❤ "I dunno how you do it! I couldn't."
- ❤ "This is only my second drink!"

I experience this defensiveness all the time—online, in person, and even when I meet someone at a party who finds out that I don't drink. People who aren't secure about their own choices take you not drinking as a referendum on them, and either defend themselves (when you didn't attack!) or use you as an armchair therapist. While it can be polite to nod along, I try to change the subject quickly. Remember, you're on a date to have fun, not discuss why your date self-medicates with alcohol to suppress their childhood trauma.

Freaked Out

- ❤ "I don't think I can date someone who doesn't drink."
- ❤ "What's the point in not drinking right now if you might drink in the future?"
- ❤ "So you can't even have *one*?"
- ❤ No response because they ghosted you.

This is a tough one. I like to think of my decision to live booze-free as a sieve that filters out the people who don't align with where I am today. Letting someone know you're not drinking may be a deal breaker for the person you're dating or matched with on an app. But again, reframing and clearly stating your boundaries can be a filter that puts you in control and lets *you* become the one who chooses to break the deal. "Someone I matched with wanted to meet for drinks. When I told him I'm not drinking right now then suggested we meet for coffee, he totally ghosted me," says Collette Astle, a New York-based singer/songwriter. "He told me months later that he assumed I had an issue with alcohol and was in AA when I said I wasn't drinking." At that point in her life, Astle had never even tasted alcohol because she grew up Mormon.

If someone freaks out and ghosts you, you can try reframing the experience. For one thing, it's their loss! Having now dated yourself, you know from experience that you're a catch. Consider also that disappearing after you share that you don't drink is hurtful and not very mature. Maybe, in addition to being their loss, it's also your gain.

Supportive

- ❤ "I've always wanted to do a dry month. Can I do it with you?"
- ❤ "Good for you. I know that can probably be challenging. Let me know if there's anything I can do to make our time together more comfortable."
- ❤ "You're so inspiring."
- ❤ "Does it bother you if I drink?"

If someone you're seeing wants to be an ally to your sobriety or sober curiosity, they probably genuinely care about you! If they ask how they can help, let them know what you need. If you don't need anything, that's OK to say, too. It's nice to leave that door open in case something pops up in the future where you do need their help. My close friends and family know that being an ally to my sobriety looks like taking the extra effort to find a restaurant with nonalcoholic drinks or understanding when I need to back out of plans because I'm not in the mood to be around alcohol.

Maybe your partner or date perks up when you tell them that you're doing a dry month and they want to do it with you! Having a sexy booze-free buddy could be a great way to explore the nonalcoholic drink scene or try some herbal aphrodisiacs (more on this later). Clear communication can keep you on the same page. Establish boundaries and ways to communicate if one of you decides to drink again.

That said, it's possible for supportive types to become a little smothering, either because they idealize you for doing something they say is inspirational or because they become overly concerned for your well-being. Feel free to tell them that they can best support your sobriety by not making it such a big deal.

Indifferent

- ❤ "Cool! Can I grab you a seltzer?"
- ❤ "I'll make sure our next date spot has some tasty nonalcoholic drinks for you."
- ❤ "Thanks for sharing that with me! I like getting to know more about you."
- ❤ "The important question is, do you want to split nachos?"

This might sound weird, but indifference is my favorite form of support. A neutral reaction means that the person I'm talking with most likely has a normal or healthy relationship with alcohol. If you're dating someone who wants to take the conversation further than "I don't drink," and you feel comfortable, that's when you can share a little bit more about your relationship with alcohol.

Just like going on a sober date or having sober sex for the first time, disclosing your booze-free status to someone else can feel overwhelming at first. This conversation should only happen when you're ready. Remember that many people don't drink for various reasons: religious affiliations, medication interactions, health conditions, and believe it or not, some people just don't like alcohol. Reevaluating your relationship with booze feels *big*—because it is! But the gravity of the "coming out" conversation speaks more to the societal pressures to imbibe than to anything about you. You're not strange or a buzzkill for taking a moment to question the role alcohol plays in your love life.

CHAPTER 3

DATING OUTSIDE THE BOX
(AND OUTSIDE THE BAR)

I recently invited one of my close friends, Aimée, over to chat about the intersection of alcohol and first dates while we split a bottle of trendy botanical extract. She's a thirty-three-year-old flight attendant who practices mindful drinking on dates. "There's so much anxiety before the date even happens," she told me. "I wonder, 'Where are we going to go? Who's going to pay? Will he judge me if I'm late because someone decides to start a fire on the 1 train?' Sometimes, I'm tired after a long work day, and alcohol can make a first date suck less." That said, she told me that someone getting drunk on the first date would be a deal breaker: "There's a big difference between enjoying a nice cocktail while getting to know each other versus needing alcohol to function or become a different version of yourself."

Aimée's not alone when it comes to examining the role alcohol plays in her dating life. The popular dating app Hinge published a survey in June 2022 where they interviewed 3,000 Gen Z (born between 1997 and 2012) and millennial (born between 1981 and 1996) global participants about what they're looking for in a date. It turns out that 75 percent of Gen Z and millennial singles are looking for a first date that's not just going to get a drink, and two-thirds say a drunk date is a deal breaker. Dry dating is even more popular among younger people—Gen Z folks are 46 percent more likely to prefer an alcohol-free date than their millennial counterparts. More than half of respondents said they were interested in dry dating because they wanted to form a genuine connection.

"Let's meet for drinks" is a standard suggestion for first dates (and often continues being the go-to date all the way through a relationship). Grabbing a drink seems like an effortless way to connect, but is effortless always a good way to approach dating? Some of that effort—the effort of getting to know someone, the effort of opening up, the effort of paying attention—is what dating, and staying together, is all about. "Alcohol suppresses parts of the brain responsible for empathy and organization," sex therapist Dr. Thomas Wood told me. "You can't connect without those parts of the brain. It's just not possible."

Dr. Wood's words helped me understand why some of my casual sober dating experiences were often more meaningful than some of my long-term drunken relationships. Even if a booze-free date didn't advance to a second date, it was usually still a kinder, more mindful connection than when I met randos in a bar. With dry dating, liquid courage is off the table, which allowed me to bring my intrinsic courage to dinner. The pressure to be "on" went down the drain along with the booze.

Lynn Macarin-Mara, the therapist who shared tips on trauma bonding in Chapter 2, has been my therapist since August 2016 (when I was nine months sober). She's heard all my sober dating stories, so naturally, I interviewed her for this book. "Dating without alcohol is cheaper and less calories," she joked with me during a phone call. More seriously, though: "If alcohol is not present, then you have a quicker chance to get to know who they are and how they handle stressful or awkward situations, and you can see them in a truer light." Seeing people, including ourselves, in a truer light is the exact point of dating without booze. This idea might feel like a challenge initially—because it is. But it gets easier. And remember, it's OK to exert a bit of effort when looking for a potential partner, celebrating a milestone, or even just having a night of fun.

So let's explore some booze-free date ideas for different relationship stages, discuss why those different stages have us reaching for the bottle, and learn how to reach for an alcohol-free alternative. You may be shocked to realize that many dates are inherently booze-free!

FIRST DATES

I met Rebekkah Rumora, a food writer and sommelier, through my partner. A mutual friend tried to set them up on a date but they became good friends instead. Even though she and her now husband both drink, they had creative booze-free first dates. "One of the first things Moritz and I bonded over after we matched on Bumble was our mutual love for photography," she shared over email. "A blizzard had just pummeled New York City so he suggested we take a photo walk through Central Park. It was the first time in years I had been asked out on a first date that didn't include meeting for drinks. There were of course first date jitters on both ends, but engaging in a shared creative activity that requires looking at things from different angles built a sort of creative, low-key intimacy between us." Once they established a solid connection, they opted to have a few beers at a sports bar. "So the date wasn't alcohol-free completely," she continues, "but the initial bonding was."

The bonding that Rebekkah and Moritz experienced solidifies Dr. Wood's earlier quote about how alcohol hinders the ability to form genuine connection. Their second date was even more endearing. They were supposed to meet at the Metropolitan Museum of Art after she walked for a few hours at the Women's March, but he ended up marching with her and her friends. "Over that seven-hour march, we realized we have a laundry list of shared values and viewed the world through a similar lens," she told me. "It wasn't the standard millennial mating ritual of 'hey, let's get drunk and fuck and then see if we like each other.' It was, 'hey, let's see if our values and interests match, and see if we enjoy each other's company enough to commit time and effort into building a relationship.'" The lack of alcohol created space for them to engage with each other in a meaningful, sustained manner. They're now married and living in Berlin. She even asked me for nonalcoholic drink suggestions to serve at their wedding!

We go on first dates because we're looking for something. Maybe it's a fun night out. Maybe it's just the ability to say that you're putting yourself out there. Maybe you're even looking for love. Whatever the reason, first dates can feel incredibly overwhelming. "Sober dating is like sober socializing but on steroids," said Amanda White, the therapist and author from Chapter 1. "Not only are you meeting a new person, having to talk to them in an intimate setting, but there is also the possibility of sexual intimacy." These anxieties are why I often reached for a drink. While alcohol may be an easy way to take the edge off, it's not the only way to make first dates less intimidating. Finding a booze-free date that addresses your particular worries can make you feel more relaxed and encourage you to tap into real courage, while also taking the temptation of alcohol off the table.

Pregaming Without the Booze

I was a big fan of "pregaming" to quell my pre-date jitters. Originally from college tailgating culture, pregaming is a ritual of drinking before social events such as parties, football games, and dates. The idea is that you'll spend less money on alcohol at the event, and maybe also start the night feeling looser. For me, pregaming allowed me to avoid having to tap into real courage before a date. Without a drink, I would spend my preparation time overthinking what to wear and what to talk about. I also spiraled into "what if they don't like me" scenarios. The only way I knew to turn off that inner monologue was to drink. Once I removed alcohol from my dates, I found that I could get that same sense of calm and preparation from other rituals, without risking being sloppy by the time my date started.

A pre-date ritual can get you in the right headspace, so you don't need to reach for a cocktail. Get in touch with your intrinsic courage before you're on the actual date!

- Drinking to feel confident? Make a pre-date playlist filled with songs that make you feel confident and flirty, or send a selfie to your bestie so they can gas you up before the big date.

- Drinking to relax? Have a cup of herbal tea while you're getting ready, or try some breathwork exercises or meditation to calm your central nervous system.

- Drinking to feel energized? A pre-date workout can get your endorphins going. Or have a cup of coffee, a caffeinated tea, or an energy drink.

Take Your Coffee to Go

While "let's meet for coffee" is technically an easy sober date suggestion, your time is still spent just sitting there, sipping cold brew and talking about yourself—and probably engaging in some kind of nervous habit like tapping your foot or voraciously picking at a nagging hangnail, because talking about yourself is one of *the* most nerve-racking parts of dating. Let's face it: dating can be awkward AF. This awkwardness is one of the many reasons why I preferred dating with alcohol. Maybe a drink took the edge off, but boozy dates rarely resulted in a genuine connection with someone. Especially since I hardly ever stopped at one drink.

Incorporating some movement, or just a change of scenery, into the date can help relieve some anxious foot-tapping and hangnail-biting energy. Maybe you take coffees to go, then sightsee around a part of town you haven't visited lately. You know that road trip game of counting out-of-state license plates? Maybe you can create a pedestrian-friendly version. For example: when someone wearing a red shirt walks by, you can share a fun fact about yourselves or take a sip of your coffee. We're replacing booze on a date, but the lighthearted fun of a drinking game can stay!

Digital Get Down

Many of us got more comfortable connecting on-screen during the COVID-19 pandemic. Video dates made meeting new people more accessible while staying safe and socially distanced. The pandemic lockdown also led to a surge in creative online activities. Virtual escape rooms, cooking classes, and group exercise classes became easily accessible if you had Wi-Fi and a screen.

I took an online pasta-making class early in the pandemic. An adorable grandmother and granddaughter in Italy taught us how to make pasta from scratch—no pasta machine required! The virtual event was technically a team-building exercise for work, but I realized how fun this experience could be for a date. After the cooking class ends, you and your date can do a virtual chat while eating your homemade pasta, laughing at the messy mistakes you made during class. Maybe your second date is cooking pasta together again, this time IRL!

Some friends and I also participated in an Alice in Wonderland–themed virtual escape room. We worked together to solve riddles which helped us advance through a series of levels until, ultimately, we "escaped." Working together to get out of pseudo dilemmas will help you get to know each other on a deeper level. Plus, the screen can serve as a barrier while you stay safe in the comfort of your own home.

Gabby Valdes, the dating coach from Chapter 2, says that virtual hangouts can be a great tool to help people feel safe on a sober date since they provide a chance to focus on the quality of connection instead of worrying about what your date might think about you. "If you go on an IRL date when you're not ready, you're actually doing a disservice to yourself and your date," Valdes shared in an email interview. "You likely won't be present. You'll overthink everything. You might even order an alcoholic drink to make them feel comfortable. Set yourself up for success by suggesting a virtual date. You'll be more comfortable and present."

Look at Art (or Flowers, or Animals . . .)

I never liked going to dinner on a first date. My BDD flared up, making me worry about how much I was eating or how I looked when I ate. Instead, I'm a fan of dates that focus on something external, like art in a museum, animals in a zoo, or flowers in a botanical garden. Exploring local scenery can create a fun, light way to connect one-on-one. This activity can also be a unique opportunity to bond over a shared affinity for a piece of artwork or fondness of an animal instead of bonding over something heavy like politics or the obligatory "What do you do for a living? Where are you from?"

There's also nothing wrong with some wholesome tourist fun. Sometimes my partner and I find a part of Manhattan we haven't explored yet and just walk around. Check your local listings for car shows, balloon races, a minor league baseball game, or anything in that realm. Take in some culture instead of taking in booze.

Embrace the Seasons

Each season brings exciting new date ideas and reasons to get outside our homes (and our heads!). Springtime dates might include cherry blossom festivals or farmers markets. It can be exciting to connect with someone while the weather changes from winter snow to fresh, blooming flowers. Replace popular boozy summertime dates such as outdoor happy hours or rosé-fueled picnics. Create your own booze-free chance to hang in the great outdoors on dates through hiking or making a kombucha-fueled picnic. Fall is a great time to replace the Oktoberfest craft beers with pumpkin carving or apple picking. You don't need booze to keep the fall vibes alive! And winter allows us to check out holiday lights or indoor markets. Swap the hot toddy for a warm apple cider.

Play Games, the Healthy Way!

Interactive dates are ideal for neurodivergent folks or anyone who feels more comfortable connecting through something participatory instead of just making conversation. Arcades are a fun way to play old-school video games like the original *Mortal Kombat* or *Donkey Kong*. Board game cafés invite you to drink coffee while playing games or working on a puzzle. You won't even realize you're not drinking because you're immersed in nostalgia or finding the right puzzle piece.

More Booze-Free First Date Ideas

- ❤ Horseback riding
- ❤ Bowling
- ❤ Cat café
- ❤ Paint your own pottery
- ❤ Coffee shop crawl
- ❤ Roller skating

Conversation Starters

I leaned on booze to avoid awkward dating moments. I had to get creative when coming up with discussion topics once I ditched booze. Here are a few classic games and ice breakers to get you through those lulls of silence on the first few dates.

TWENTY QUESTIONS

This is a spoken game where one of you thinks of something random—a cat? A taco? The *Seinfeld* diner? Then the other person has twenty yes-or-no questions to figure out what's on your mind.

THREE FICTIONAL CHARACTERS

In 2015, there was a social media trend where people made a photo collage of three fictional characters representing their personality. Mine included Ilana Wexler (Ilana Glazer's character on *Broad City*), Chris Traeger (Rob Lowe's character on *Parks and Recreation*), and Leslie Knope (Amy Poehler's character on *Parks and Recreation*). Sidenote: can you guess what my favorite TV show is? Challenge your date to pick three characters and explain what aspects of themselves those characters represent, then do the same for yourself.

FUCK, MARRY, KILL

Name three celebrities. Your date has to choose one to fuck, one to marry, and one to kill. Get weird by bringing in random cartoon characters, fast food chains, or team mascots.

DESERT ISLAND PICKS

You've probably played this game before. Which album/TV show/movie/book would you take with you if you were stranded on a desert island? Remove the realism of needing electricity to watch your favorite shows or listen to your favorite albums (and the fact that you'd have to plan on being stranded). Sharing your desert island picks can say a lot about you and help you learn more about your person, too!

DREAM SCENARIOS

- Which historical figure would you invite to dinner and what's on the menu?

- Which reality TV star would you like to spend the day with and which activity are y'all doing?

- Which game show would you like to be a contestant on and what's the big prize that you walk away with?

DATING

This stage is when you're seeing someone regularly. You're not quite talking about the next big step (moving in together, marriage, matching tattoos), but you've met each other's friends, and maybe you've even met their family. While there's a certain comfort in being at this level, some stressors still arise which can seem much easier to deal with while sipping a martini. You might be wondering: *What's next? Are they the one? Is monogamy for me? Is their cynicism a deal breaker? Am I just looking for deal breakers to prevent getting my heart broken again because that last breakup was so devastating why the hell am I even dating in the first place?!* Before that downward spiral leads to a carafe of Aperol spritz, let's explore some fun we're-super-into-each other dates that don't include alcohol.

Tea and Chill

I'm obsessed with coffee as my daily productivity bestie, but I also love tea for its nuanced flavor profiles and relaxing, medicinal properties. If you live somewhere with a tea garden, 100 percent go there on a date! It's easier to feel calm in a place designed for relaxation. If you don't live near a tea garden, any tea house will provide a more mellow vibe than a coffee shop's cacophony of smooth jazz and grinding coffee beans while a barista calls out, "Britney, iced oat milk latte!"

There's something endearing about sharing a pot of tea with a person I care about. Some traditional tea houses provide space to sit on the floor, creating a unique, cozy date experience. Chat with each other about the tea you're drinking while you take in the aroma and savor the different flavors. These mindful practices can keep you feeling present and grounded instead of mindlessly taking two-for-one tequila shots.

Where coffee has the "get shit done" vibe, tea has the "slow shit down" vibe. And it's not just a vibe; it's the L-theanine, an amino acid that naturally occurs in green and black teas. It calms the nervous system, which is exactly what you may want while on a sober date.

Work Out

One time I had a job interview for an athleisure brand that included something the company called a sweat date. This meant meeting my potential new boss for a group fitness class. The job was more than selling stretchy pants; they also wanted their employees to connect with the local fitness community while wearing our signature spandex. I liked the idea of a sweat date, so I brought it into my sober dating experiences.

On sweat dates, I didn't feel as bummed if there wasn't a spark because we still had fun at hot yoga or indoor rock climbing. Maybe that's my type-A Capricorn energy that makes me love efficiency. Either way, exercising together was a great way to release that "OMG, I'm on a date!" anxious fidgeting.

My partner and I still enjoy practicing yoga together. I don't think I had any shared, healthy hobbies with past partners when I still drank. Not a big fitness buff? Implement some not-so-exercise-y movement through mini golf or paintball.

Go Shopping

A bookstore date is an introvert's dream! You can browse sections together, showing each other the type of books you like or are looking forward to reading. You can also be adventurous by picking a book for each other. Designate a meeting place, then agree to be there with a book in hand for the other person. This is a cute way to share a little bit of yourself with someone you like. Plus, discussing each other's book selection makes for charming in-between-dates text fodder. Similarly, you can apply the same approach to a greeting card store or flower shop. You'll be so busy with the excitement of picking out a cute gift and anticipating what your gift is that you won't even realize that there's no booze.

A similarly creative vibe and even more sustainable experience could be going to a vintage clothing store, a record store, or a consignment shop. Give each other fifteen minutes to find a random gift for each other. (It's nice to support small businesses if you can, but if you're being mindful about money, you don't even have to buy it! Just point out something that you think the other person would like.) Again, it's a fun way to spend your time together while also securing a second date or maybe even taking the date back to your apartment. Who needs alcohol when you're busy listening to a classic Nina Simone record?

Try a Booze-Free Nightcap

I never thought I'd hear the words *sober bar*, but it's a thing! The first time my partner and I went to Listen Bar, a pop-up alcohol-free bar, he said, "It feels nice to have a second stop after a dinner date." I didn't even realize I missed stopping for a nightcap until he expressed it. It's not that I missed after-dinner cocktails, but I missed having a second activity before we went home. These hot spots are popping up all over the globe. The clientele is there to socialize without booze and the bartender makes tasty drinks that don't need alcohol. Check online for lists of sober bars and bottle shops to see if there's one in your area.

SAY WHAT? SOBER BAR

It looks just like a "normal" bar: bartenders standing in front of a stocked bar, people clinking glasses to celebrate a big win, while contemporary music sets the vibe. But all of the sophisticated drinks are alcohol-free.

Sometimes, when a date goes well, you may want to invite them up for a drink (and then some!). Just because booze may not be an option right now doesn't mean that nightcaps are off the table. Try stocking a few tasty nonalcoholic options in your fridge or pantry. Many liquor stores and grocery stores now carry some yummy nonalcoholic beverages, and many drinks are available to purchase online. Nonalcoholic drinks range from zero-proof spirits to botanical blends to CBD seltzers. Chances are, your date may not be up to date on the ever-expanding nonalcoholic drink scene, so they might be impressed that you have something fun to sip on while keeping the vibe going. It can be nice to end the night with something other than seltzer.

My partner and I have a fully stocked "bar" so we can make a booze-free old-fashioned, mojito, or margarita. There are also some delicious zero-alcohol beers out there. Try having a date over for a nonalcoholic beer flight or kombucha tasting, or pop a bottle of nonalcoholic rosé to celebrate good news. If substitute booze isn't your thing, your second stop might look like having dessert at a different restaurant than your dinner or sitting in the park with a pint of ice cream.

More Booze-Free Date Ideas for Semi-Serious Relationships

- 💜 Live entertainment (drag shows, comedy shows, concerts, story slams)
- 💜 Host a game night
- 💜 Do a puzzle
- 💜 Anything from the first dates section—there's no time limit on these!

YOU MET THE ONE(S)

At this stage, you're officially in a relationship. Maybe you're cohabiting or engaged or married or have an adorable fur baby/human baby/stunning plant collection together. Whatever you're doing, you're overall pretty happy with the person or persons in your life. This happiness doesn't mean that stress goes away. Life still happens on life's terms, making a boozy date night sound tempting.

Your relationship doesn't exist in a vacuum. You're now juggling household chores and career changes, grieving loved ones, and cleaning up baby poop (or animal poop, or . . . plant poop?) while actively avoiding the twenty-four-hour news cycle. But the bonus is that you have a life partner along for the ride. Sometimes a date night looks like ordering takeout while streaming that new show everyone's tweeting about because anything more just feels like another thing on a to-do list. I get it. We're all busy. So how do we keep alcohol-free dating fun and the romance alive when we're too tired to put on pants? All the dates in the previous sections still apply once you're at this relationship stage. Only, now that you're more comfortable, you can take the dates a bit deeper.

Reignite the Passion

One of the most common complaints from folks in long-term relationships is "I miss the passion!" We'll talk about maintaining the spark in bed in Chapter 10, but sex isn't the only way you can express passion—and connecting with your intrinsic courage can also help you get in touch (in a healthy way) with other intense, authentic passionate feelings. Like rage! One time, when my partner was stressed about work, I surprised him with a random date night. I told him to meet me on 35th and 9th wearing clothes he didn't mind getting dirty. Then we walked into The Wrecking Club and raged. Literally. My playlist of Rage Against the Machine and Nine Inch Nails blared through the speakers while we smashed computer monitors, video game consoles, and printers with various crowbars and baseball bats. They also gave us a bucket of dishes to smash against the wall. We walked out onto the Manhattan streets afterward, drenched in sweat, feeling more zen than after a yoga class. We were physically exhausted and emotionally at peace. Living a life without alcohol, even sporadically, means that you probably feel your feelings way more than when you drank. Experiential dates like rage rooms and ax throwing are a great way to release that aggression. Check online to see if there's one near you.

Attending a political rally, city council meeting, or protest is another way to bond over shared passions. Remember Rebekkah and Moritz's second date at the Women's March? It's never too late to experience a monumental event like this together. Nick and I vote in all elections, especially local ones. We research the politicians running for office in our neighborhood and discuss where they stand on the issues that matter most to us. Then we walk to the voting booths together, doing our part to contribute to democracy. Passion changes over time, just like we do.

Explore Something New

Another recurring theme when a relationship gets comfortable is that we often feel like we've run out of topics to discuss, or we already know everything about each other. Spice things up by trying something new! Explore a new neighborhood by walking around, browsing local shops, and trying a new restaurant. If you're feeling adventurous, try a type of cuisine that's new to both of you. Never eaten with your hands? Try Ethiopian food or Malaysian food. Interested in pushing the boundaries of your spice tolerance? Go to a hot sauce shop to try different levels of heat. Some nonalcoholic breweries host beer tastings or let you tour the site! A deck of conversation cards can be another fun way to keep learning about each other.

You can also learn something new together, as a team. You've committed to each other, so why not commit to a series of classes? Take a foreign language course and write love notes to each other in the language you're learning. Take a pottery class where you can each make something memorable to put in your home. Maybe you've always talked about doing yoga teacher training or completing a scuba diving certification. Why not sign up to become certified together? Even if you never use your training, you'll still grow together as a team, sharing a fun, educational experience.

Netflix and Chill—With a Twist

In the opening scene of the 2017 film *Lady Bird*, Lady Bird (Saoirse Ronan) and her mom (Laurie Metcalf) listen to the audiobook version of *The Grapes of Wrath* while on a road trip. The tape finishes, then Lady Bird turns on the radio. Her mom stops her, requesting that they sit with what they just heard. "We don't have to constantly entertain ourselves, do we?" she asks. Binge drinking and binge watching are similar in that both sometimes come from this instinct to be constantly entertaining yourself, so you're never alone with your sober thoughts. But what if instead of mindlessly streaming a show with your loved one, you tried . . . well, mindfully streaming it?

Instead of letting the streaming service roll right into the next episode, press pause, then talk to each other about what you just watched. What stood out to you? Did a particular scene remind you of something? Did watching a baking show give you the sudden urge to bake cookies? Go to the store and buy the ingredients to bake those macarons together! Or maybe you really just want to watch the next episode—that's fine, too. The point here is to give yourselves the space to process what you just observed, then share those thoughts with your beloved.

Try making a collaborative playlist on your favorite music streaming app for a screen-free version of this activity. You can each contribute songs you're into, sharing why you added each song or reminiscing on the memories that certain songs bring up. Listen to this playlist on road trips or while you're playing a board game. Or, as another alternative, start a book club for two!

Get Scent-ual

We've already talked about how alcohol dulls your senses, so why not create a new sensory experience to connect with your beloved? My BFF, Jacob, and his partner, Jefferson, celebrated four years together by designing a custom cologne at a store in New York City. (This process is also available online!) First, agree on the base scent that feels foundational to both of you as a team. Second, select the core scent that elevates that foundation. Finally, customize your new cologne or perfume's name, color, and label. Who needs booze to connect when you have a unique olfactory experience?

Flirtatious Competition

A little flirtatious competition can be a fun form of booze-free foreplay. A few Thanksgivings ago, our friends Auberth and Sarang came over with two servings of mac and cheese—each following different recipes but only they knew who made which. All attendees tasted both dishes, then had to vote for which mac and cheese recipe they liked better. Auberth and Sarang bonded while making the dishes, and our other dinner guests had fun tasting and voting. If you like cooking, try your version of this! Maybe you do something similar when attending a potluck-style meal. Or turn your favorite food show into your own kitchen event and invite some friends over to be the judges. (P.S. Sarang won.)

If you're into physical competition, you can sign up for a 5k run and then playfully compete against each other while also raising money for a good cause. Or maybe arm wrestling or leg wrestling can lead to another form of physical fun. No need to have a drink to get in the mood when your endorphins are pumping!

Build a Sex Room

Netflix's 2022 show *How to Build a Sex Room* shows couples in the Denver area who've hired an interior designer to create, you guessed it, a sex room in their home. The risqué show depicts all types of relationships and explores how having a space designed specifically for pleasure improves these couples' love lives. Sex swings and butt plugs aside, it's a show about people learning how to communicate with each other while exploring their own sexual desires. As we've seen in previous chapters, communication and reevaluating your relationship with alcohol often go hand in hand.

Whether or not you and your partner or partners build a physical sex room, fantasizing about what's inside your ideal fun room can still be a vulnerable, sexy act in and of itself. Discuss what sex and pleasure mean to you and your relationship. Maybe your ideal fun room is more focused on romance or relaxation, or simply a space away from kids and laptops. Just the idea of having a small space, even the corner of a bedroom, designed for pleasure can create a sexy vibe.

More Date Ideas for When You've Found the One(s)

- ❤ Volunteer
- ❤ Go to a cultural festival
- ❤ Walk dogs
- ❤ Paddleboard or kayak or surf
- ❤ Fuck like rabbits
- ❤ Take a trip
- ❤ Dress up for the hell of it
- ❤ Cosplay at a convention
- ❤ Shoot hoops in the park
- ❤ Go for a long drive or a long walk

By now you've probably realized that there's nothing about dating that inherently requires booze. We associate dating with alcohol because that's often the first line of defense in addressing our anxieties and finding the (liquid) courage to open up to someone new. But by choosing booze-free dates that are mindful, unconventional, and focused on active connection instead of passive consumption, we don't have to rely on alcohol to quell anxieties—and we can probably have an even better time.

CHAPTER 4

EMOTIONAL INTIMACY WITHOUT ALCOHOL

I carried a Winnie-the-Pooh blankie with me everywhere as a kid. I called it my Wooby. Mom knew I couldn't eat or sleep without my makeshift invisibility cloak near me. That over-washed blanket, which eventually wore down to shreds, losing all signs that the fabric once contained Winnie and the gang, helped me feel safe. I eventually outgrew that literal security blanket, then transferred a similar attachment to alcohol years later at age sixteen. Anytime I wanted to attempt something that required even the smallest amount of bravery, I reached for booze. Alcohol quickly became my go-to when I wanted something external to quiet my internal dread. I liked that alcohol made me feel confident. Or more accurately, alcohol made me *believe* it gave me the courage to try something new. In fact, it was just a security blanket I could hang onto while accessing my intrinsic courage—but I didn't realize that courage was in me all along.

I brought my metaphorical new Wooby to every sexual experience from age sixteen to my late twenties. Drinking was so ingrained in my sexuality that it never felt like a question of whether or not to consume, but which drink am I going to have? Alcohol was always there, along for the ride, often steering the wheel.

Even when I wasn't drinking, alcohol was still in my system. Any time I wanted to have a vulnerable discussion with a partner or try something new in bed, it felt nice to have alcohol there with me, symbolically holding my hand in the same way that my Wooby once did. "When somebody believes that their sexuality can only be accessed through a substance, then it gives that substance a whole lot of power in their lives. It now owns their sexuality. It teaches them one vital lesson: that your sexuality doesn't belong to you," Dr. Wood, the sex therapist from Chapter 3, told me. Embracing my sexuality without alcohol helped establish emotional intimacy by connecting me to my authentic self.

In a world forcing you to move faster, do more, and share it publicly on social media, it can feel like your sex should also be, as the Kings of Leon say, "on fire." But what if you slowed down enough to explore how emotional intimacy with less (or no!) alcohol might improve your love, sex, and dating life?

Emotional intimacy is a true bond that organically forms from trust and communication. Within that trust lives a layer of vulnerability that makes connecting emotionally terrifying to some (me!). I don't think I could have experienced emotional intimacy until I learned how to empathize. Emotional intimacy works both ways. It's when people see and embrace each other for who they are.

EMOTIONAL SOBRIETY

Emotional sobriety is a lesser-known term, but the concept is implemented in most therapies and recovery spaces. It means getting honest about your emotions, letting yourself process the full range of your feelings without reaching for something (alcohol, people, gambling) to numb the discomfort.

My friend Ceasar F. Barajas, a Navy veteran and meditation instructor, first told me about emotional sobriety early in my own recovery journey. "I found myself getting angry. That anger turned into aggression because I felt unsafe. My anger was essentially a protection mechanism," he told me. "I went through the twelve steps, the first time, while living in LA in 2011. It was 'Hi, I'm Ceasar and I am powerless over my emotions.' Those meetings were full of folks who don't have a grasp on their feelings. Sobriety isn't confined solely to substances." Talking with Ceasar about emotions felt refreshing; he gives me hope that people, especially men, really *want* to manage their emotions while also being a mindful partner.

"My ongoing hourly maintenance of emotional sobriety gives me awareness that I've never had before when going into a partnership," Ceasar told me. "I know now that I don't need seven drinks to build up the confidence to explore with a partner. When I'm speaking to a potential lover, I tell them up front what I deal with. My anxieties, my depression, my post-traumatic stress injuries. And it isn't a daily struggle. It's hourly." Getting in touch with his emotions helps Ceasar respectfully communicate his sexual desires as well. "I'll tell them, 'I'm interested in pegging. Would you go on this adventure with me?'" Communicating from a space of safety and peace helps Ceasar experience healthy boundaries with clear expectations so he and his partner can feel emotionally and physically safe. "I am finally confident in *me*, first," he concludes.

I drank excessively to attempt the impossible task of numbing my emotional pain while enjoying physical pleasure. Except I ended up numbing everything, creating artificial fun and dangerous situations. "We cannot selectively numb emotions," Brené Brown, the queen of vulnerability, reminds us in her 2010 book, *The Gifts of Imperfection*. "When we numb the painful emotions, we also numb the positive emotions." Selective numbing only happens with local anesthesia in the doctor's or dentist's office—there's no emotional equivalent. You make yourself open to feeling everything, or you feel nothing.

Drinking less alcohol while reconnecting with my emotions led to discovering one of the many reasons I mixed alcohol and sex in the first place: emotional intimacy scared the hell out of me. This is a common pattern—people who are afraid of being vulnerable, often because of underlying anxiety or trauma, turn to physical intimacy to avoid their feelings, to avoid having hard conversations, to avoid being honest with themselves or someone else. And they turn to alcohol to make it easier to detach that physical intimacy from emotional intimacy. This may be especially true for people from historically marginalized communities who are shouldering cultural or racial trauma on top of individual stressors. "I have found that when we, as queer people, enter recovery, we often recover more than sobriety," wrote Tracey Anne Duncan in a 2022 Mic.com article. "It was in the process of recovery that I fully embraced my gender nonconformity, and it was in recovery support groups that I learned the emotional skills I needed to have nurturing relationships. In other words, getting sober is as much about getting clean with yourself about yourself as it is about kicking a drug." Duncan's words echo Ceasar's sentiments about emotional sobriety. Learning how to process your emotions without alcohol helps establish emotional intimacy, whether in long-term recovery or while being sober curious. Exploring emotional intimacy without booze helped me get comfortable with eye contact, hand holding, and more that will come up later in the book.

BOOZE, THE WORST THREESOME PARTNER

Simone Finch's 2022 television show *Single Drunk Female*, loosely based on Finch's life, follows Sam, a single woman under thirty, as she learns to navigate life and relationships without alcohol. The first season has a powerful scene where Sam confides in her sponsor that she feels anxious about having sober sex for the first time. Her sponsor delivers the iconic line, "You just have to get used to being in your body. You never had to before because you were always having a threesome with booze."

Watching *Single Drunk Female* at six years sober helped me reflect on my past drunken hookups, seeing the invasive space that alcohol took up in my bed. My bed was pretty damn crowded; no wonder there wasn't room for my actual courage.

I chatted with Finch to learn more about this threesome line. "I knew that alcohol was impeding me from connecting with the people I was sleeping with," she told me. "But I also knew for a long time that I wanted that distance between me and the person . . . until I didn't." Maybe you connect sex with alcohol for the same reasons that Finch and I did: to avoid emotional intimacy. Let's explore ways to discover emotional intimacy in sobriety or sober curiosity. Hint: start with your friends!

GET EMOTIONALLY INTIMATE WITH YOUR FRIENDS FIRST

You don't have to dive right into emotional intimacy with potential partners to practice being vulnerable and open. It's important to remember that emotional intimacy shows up with your friends and family, too. Nurturing your friendships and your relationship with yourself will make it easier to nurture relationships with your dates or partners. When I was drinking, I kept my friends emotionally at arm's length by hiding behind alcohol and sex, feeling more comfortable sharing graphic sexual details than the vulnerable, emotional aspects of my relationships. Giving up drinking and gaining the capacity for emotional intimacy allowed me to pursue deeper friendships and, ultimately, deeper romantic relationships. Before you make room for emotional intimacy with a partner, take stock of how emotional intimacy shows up in your friendships.

It may look like the following:

- ❤ Rituals: Do you have a standing date with a friend? Maybe you meet for coffee every Friday to transition from work week to weekend. Or you text each other while watching *The Bachelor* every week.

- ❤ Secret language: Do you and your BFF have code words, inside jokes, or slang that only the two of you know? Maybe you have a specific look or a nod representing "it's time to go!"

💜 Seeing the real you: Who's the one person who can drop by unannounced, or who you don't have to tidy up for? Someone who's probably seen you at your physical and emotional worst? That's the friend you have emotional intimacy with.

💜 ICE: Maybe your BFF is your In Case of Emergency contact.

These are emotionally intimate relationships that organically formed and are sustained because you're authentic with each other. You call them when shit hits the fan. You tell them how you feel, 100 percent unfiltered with no liquid courage needed. These are the relationships that you put time and energy into nurturing. This is the buddy you can talk about your sobriety or sober curiosity with. Maybe they'll even be a guinea pig for some of your practice convos before you attempt sober dating!

Don't count on your partner to fulfil all your emotional needs. This is why you need time to date yourself, and your friends! Drunk me liked having dozens of "friends," but sober me realizes that I can only show up correctly for a handful of relationships at a time.

When you find *the one* (or if you already have), remember to nurture your friendships, too.

HOW TO BRING EMOTIONAL INTIMACY INTO SOBER DATING

It can be difficult to find the sweet spot of vulnerability versus oversharing, just like it can be difficult to find balance with drinking. Getting drunk to calm my nerves on a first date often left me with regrets and a headache the next morning. But soberly oversharing left me with an emotional hangover that hurt just as much as a booze-induced one. When I stopped dulling my emotions with alcohol, I would overcorrect and wind up spilling my guts—because I wasn't actually ready to be emotionally open, and oversharing *looked* like openness without feeling as risky. Just as you need to get in touch with your intrinsic courage instead of reaching for the easy fix of alcohol, you can learn to access genuine vulnerability instead of feeling compelled to overshare. Being present and learning more about each other at your own pace removes much of the drama and creates a deeper connection.

Vulnerability is a bridge that helps people connect through shared intimacy and emotional intelligence, while oversharing is more like a traffic jam on said bridge. Oversharing might be a sign of a lack of boundaries or missing self-awareness, which often leaves the listener feeling alienated or perplexed by what was just shared.

I used to think that emotional intimacy meant pouring your heart out on the first date. Now I see those moments as a version of oversharing. It felt strange to let dates or partners discover facets of me organically instead of sprinkling my past traumas over the appetizers. I felt like it was my responsibility to fill those awkward silences, so I reverted to, "Here's some shit that happened to me." Now I'd fill those silences with discussing the show I just binged or a book I'm currently reading. Or realize that it's not my responsibility to fill those silences at all.

VULNERABILITY	OVERSHARING
Telling difficult personal stories, but letting people know you'll stop if they're uncomfortable or feel like you're sharing too much.	Starting a sentence with "This is TMI, but . . ." and continuing anyway.
Taking time to breathe, gauge the person's reaction, and give them a chance to ask questions or ask you to stop.	Telling your story in one breath.
Disclosing that you are in recovery or rethinking your relationship with alcohol.	Telling your rock-bottom story right away.
Poking fun at yourself for weird habits or small mistakes.	Compulsively putting yourself down or apologizing.
"Sometimes it takes me a bit longer to open up as I navigate getting to know someone."	"I have daddy issues and tend not to trust men because I've been fucked over so many times in the past!"
"I really like your energy and enjoy being around you."	"Wanna fuck?"

Keep in mind that these examples are just that: examples. In some interactions, it might be perfectly acceptable to discuss rehab details, share a TMI story, or confidently ask if your date wants to have sex. Vulnerability means different things to different people. And that definition may evolve the longer you stay on a booze-free journey. Take time to check in with yourself as you experience moments of sharing with someone; what might feel right with one person could look vastly different with another. Notice how you feel as it's happening, and perhaps consider these simple questions: Do I feel safe? Is this person holding space for me to be myself? Does sharing this detail feel important in this moment?

Like anything in life, but especially sober dating, vulnerability will always benefit from a little mindfulness.

EMOTIONAL INTIMACY IN ACTION

If you're newly learning how to open up to people and achieve emotional intimacy, it can help to start small. You don't have to jump straight to your biggest fears, dreams, or disappointments. Instead, try discussing how you feel about something low-stakes, like a movie you just watched or your hot take on that viral article everyone's reading. This allows you to discuss your emotions while also holding the door open for them to share theirs. Getting comfortable with sharing emotional intimacy around lighter topics might make it easier to discuss heavier topics as the relationship gets deeper. As your connection grows over time, so will your emotional intimacy. Plus, you've each laid the groundwork for being OK with discussing emotions.

INSTEAD OF: I love how that movie ended!

TRY: The ending of that movie made me feel _____. It reminded me of _____.

Vulnerably expressing how a shared experience made you feel can also be a great opportunity to discuss what you're looking for in a relationship or a partner. There's an unspoken pressure these days to be "the cool girl." Women who date men are supposed to act like we don't care about texting or phone calls or if the hookup meant something. Somehow, it became too demanding to put "looking for love" on a dating app, but it's still acceptable for men to state their fetishes, sexual desires, and expectations. Hopefully one day both ideas can merge, making it socially acceptable to put "looking for love . . . and butt stuff."

INSTEAD OF: Pretending like you're OK with minimal communication between dates

TRY: "I love texting you about my day between our dates. I also like hearing about your day."

It's OK to text them and to want them to text! The "wait three days to call" rule is a relic of the past. If you want to talk to someone, talk to them. I stopped playing those games when I quit drinking—partly because I hate wasting my time, but also because I learned it's OK to admit I like someone and that I want them to reciprocate that feeling.

INSTEAD OF: Pretending to be in a good mood after having a shitty day when they ask how you're doing

TRY: "Honestly, not great. Had a terrible day at work. But seeing your name pop up on my phone made me smile!"

These small forays into emotional honesty show someone that you're opening up about your life, and hold space for them to do the same. Conversations like this keep the emotional intimacy growing; no alcohol required!

INSTEAD OF: Pretending to like seafood when your date suggests sushi for dinner

TRY: "I'm not a big fan of seafood. How about Italian? There's a seafood option for you and I'll just get pasta."

Pretending to like something that you dislike just to avoid rocking the boat might be emblematic of people-pleasing. And those tendencies most likely show up elsewhere (ahem: like in bed) Unapologetically stating that you don't like seafood lets your date learn about the things you don't like while also possibly giving you a nudge of confidence to advocate for yourself elsewhere.

HOW TO DATE SOMEONE WHO DRINKS

Dating someone who drinks when you're sober or sober curious can present some not-so-fun emotional hurdles and awkward conversations. You get to establish the alcohol boundaries that are best for your mental health, but that doesn't always keep someone else from feeling judged by that boundary. (The first step, though, is to make sure that you're *not* judging them for having a different relationship with alcohol than you. Remember that people drink for various reasons. Just because you're taking a break from booze right now doesn't mean everyone else is taking a break or needs to.)

During my years of sober dating in Manhattan, most of the people I met drank socially. Many of these folks seemed to know a magic trick I never learned: responsible drinking. I'm still in awe when I see someone leave a pint glass of beer on the table, half full, or they slowly sip the liquor in a shot glass. Where did they learn how to do that?!

Some dates drank in a way that made me feel uncomfortable. These interactions rarely went past one or two dates because I realized that dating someone who got wasted regularly was incredibly triggering for me. That's when I learned how to set boundaries around dating people who drink alcohol—it wasn't about whether their drinking was a problem for *them*, but whether they made sobriety more difficult for me. Remember that it's not up to you to decide if someone else has a drinking problem or if they drink too much. It's up to you to know if someone's drinking makes you feel uneasy or hinders your ability to make your own choices.

That's why it's helpful to know what you're comfortable with when dating someone who drinks—and it's also helpful to keep checking in on that comfort level. For example, you may think you can't date someone who drinks, but your perspective may shift when you click with someone who enjoys a glass of wine with dinner and you see that they almost never have a second. On the flip side, you may think you're cool with a date who drinks any amount, but then find that dating someone who regularly has multiple beers back to back makes it too hard to resist cracking one yourself. Your boundary is allowed to change over time.

COMMUNICATE YOUR BOUNDARIES

Here are a few sample sentences to communicate your boundaries when dating or in a relationship with someone who drinks:

❤ If kissing someone with boozy breath turns you off or makes you rethink your sobriety/sober curiosity: "Would you mind brushing your teeth before we have some sexy time? The smell of whiskey is a little triggering for me."

❤ If going to a restaurant with a bar makes you feel uneasy: "I'd rather not eat at restaurants that serve alcohol right now. How about we try that new frozen yogurt spot for dessert after I cook dinner?"

❤ If you don't want alcohol in the house: "I know you like a glass of wine when you get home, but I'm struggling with having alcohol within reach. I'd love to discuss ways we can both feel supported in our house."

❤ If you attend a party but want to leave once people get rowdy: "This party looks fun! I may leave if the alcohol gets too much, but feel free to stay if you want and just meet me at home."

❤ If they come home drunk after a night with their friends: "I'm so glad you had fun! I'm going to finish this TV show before bed. See you in the morning!"

❤ If they're intoxicated and want to have sex with you: "I love being intimate with you when we're both fully present. Let's wait until tomorrow."

❤ If they try to explain your sobriety/sober curiosity to people you may not know too well: "I appreciate your enthusiasm about my decision not to drink right now. In the future, I'd rather be the one to bring up my sobriety in a group setting."

IDENTIFY YOUR DEAL BREAKERS

Setting boundaries around alcohol in your relationship can also help you figure out what your deal breakers are. Here are a few personal deal breakers I discovered while dating sober:

- ❤ Dating profile photos where the person holds a drink were an immediate swipe left. Maybe I was being hypersensitive, but people choose what they're presenting in their dating profiles and I didn't like feeling that they were leading with alcohol.

- ❤ I don't feel comfortable around something I call "the glaze"—that point of intoxication when you can practically see the inhibitions leave someone's body as their eyes glaze over. I couldn't date anyone who drank to that level on a regular basis.

- ❤ I'm fine with meeting someone in a bar, but the minute a date disrespected the bartender, I was out. Feeling entitled to special treatment because of who you are or who you know signals assholery that I have no interest in being part of.

These may be deal breakers for you, or they may not—neither is wrong! You'll have your own hard lines. But as you're considering your boundaries around drinking, it's worth figuring out what behaviors are intolerable for you—just like you would with any other aspect of your dating life. Drinking is normalized and expected in American culture, which can make it harder to set boundaries; you may feel pressure not only to drink, but to excuse any and all drinking behavior from others. But you're allowed to have a comfort zone and stick to it, even if your deal breakers would be unremarkable to someone else. That's as true for drinking as it is for any other category of behavior.

SIGNS THAT YOU SHOULDN'T DATE A DRINKER

If any of the following feelings arise, it might be time to reevaluate your boundaries when dating someone who drinks. Some of these emotional shifts can be super subtle. Check in with yourself regularly to catch any changes in your feelings early on.

- ❤ When they drink, you fantasize about sharing that drink with them.

- ❤ After a date, you feel a little off the next day. Did watching them drink make you feel uncomfortable? Did it make you miss drinking?

- ❤ You feel resentment, jealousy, or annoyance about the other person's drinking.

- ❤ You wonder if this whole not-drinking thing is pointless. Maybe you convince yourself that you should have "just one."

- ❤ You compare your relationship to alcohol with how they drink.

- ❤ Tasting the alcohol on their breath after a kiss leaves you craving booze.

If you notice any of the following, their drinking may also be a problem for you—but just because they're an asshole:

- ❤ They try to get you to drink after you've made it clear that you're not drinking right now.

- ❤ They incorporate alcohol into most dates and social settings even after you told them it makes you uncomfortable.

- ❤ They tease you, either alone or supposedly jokingly in front of their friends, about not drinking.

- They become a different, unpleasant person after a few drinks.

- Their drinking seems to accelerate after a few drinks.

- They're unaware of or indifferent to their problematic behavior the following morning.

- Said indifference leads to them gaslighting you for being concerned or hurt by their actions.

IF YOU'RE ALREADY IN A RELATIONSHIP

You have your own relationship with alcohol and your own reasons for drinking or not drinking. Remember that when talking about alcohol with your partner—the most important thing you can do is respect their reasons and share your own. Honesty and communication will be the most important factors in weathering any relationship change, including a change in your feelings about alcohol.

My friend Taylor is a thirty-one-year-old lawyer and mother based in Tulsa, whose husband, Caleb, is in recovery from alcohol use disorder. Taylor's what I would call a normie. She's someone who has a healthy, moderate relationship with alcohol. She can take it or leave it. I talked with her about how she shows up for Caleb's sobriety. "When my husband first got sober, and we were both figuring out our role in the whole process, I sat in on some phone-conference Al-Anon meetings, but it wasn't the right fit," she told me. "However, I did follow some subreddits for people like me, people who love someone with alcohol use disorder, and people like Caleb, who identify as a person with alcohol use disorder." Reading the testimonies of others provided Taylor with insight. She even picked up some common recovery lingo which helps Caleb feel supported. "It helped me find my own connection without constantly bothering my husband to let me into his head," she concluded.

SAY WHAT? NORMIE

Someone who has a healthy, moderate relationship with alcohol. Someone who can drink alcohol without their personality changing or ending up in dangerous situations.

Not all partners are as thoughtful as Taylor, at least at first. Tension may arise if you're in a relationship and one person decides to cut back on booze while the other keeps drinking. Sometimes alcohol can be the common bond in a relationship, leaving the person who still drinks feeling rejected when their partner chooses to give up booze. I spoke with Kate Zander, a cohost of the *Seltzer Squad* podcast, about how her decision to stop drinking impacted her marriage. "In early sobriety, my husband made me feel like a wet blanket in our friend group," she said. "It's not that he was overindulging with his drinking, it's more that our lifestyles just weren't matching up. I felt let down that he wasn't excited to be hangover-free on a Saturday morning like I was." It can be difficult when your partner doesn't match the energy of something you're excited about, like waking up feeling refreshed and not hungover, or all the money you save from not buying alcohol. Again, this is where communication comes in.

"It's been a lot of years of hard conversations. We had to really be honest about how the other person's behavior impacts us," Kate continued. "I don't think he understood how to be an ally in my sobriety until I was a few years sober. His turning point was when he started therapy, and his therapist could point out how big of a deal it was for me to get sober. He had to realize that I was really working my ass off to stay sober." Kate's and Taylor's stories are why I recommend Al-Anon, CoDA (Co-Dependents Anonymous), or online research to drinking partners of a newly sober person—it may seem extreme if you don't identify as having alcohol use disorder, but these support groups are helpful for understanding how much effort you're putting into not drinking, and how much real courage it can take.

IF THEIR DRINKING IS A PROBLEM

I often hear folks say, "If my partner could just stop drinking, everything could be so much better." While I can see how removing alcohol might improve certain relationship dynamics, abstinence is just one part of the equation. Alcohol abuse is often treated as the problem when it's usually a symptom of a problem. My alcohol abuse stemmed from trying to self-medicate anxiety, depression, and PTSD, specifically sexual PTSD. And after I ditched alcohol, my underlying mental health issues were still there. In fact, I felt my feelings much more since I was no longer numbing out.

I bring all of this up to remind people whose partners still drink that you can't do their work for them—and they can't do your work for you. If it's hard for you to stay sober when your partner drinks, you can ask them to quit, or do a dry month with you, and see how they feel about it—but you can't make them do it, and if they do, it will only be part of the solution. It's also essential that both of you continue to do emotional work, including understanding why their drinking is a challenge for you, or why your sobriety is a challenge for them. Finding a therapist, peer support group, or accountability buddy can help you explore these topics on a deeper level.

There's a fine line between wanting to help someone and trying to fix them. The former comes from a place of love and concern, while the latter often comes from codependency. It's not up to you to decide if someone else has a problematic relationship with alcohol, but it is up to you to establish boundaries around their drinking, then communicate said boundaries. Don't be afraid to use those sample convos from earlier in the chapter.

DON'T	DO
Count their drinks	If necessary, tell them (when they're *not* drinking) how their drinking made you feel
Manage how much time they spend at the bar	Stay home, then let them know how their nightly happy hours make you feel
Argue with a drunk person	Take a deep breath, write down how you feel, then let them know in the morning

Here are some additional nuggets to keep in mind when dealing with a partner whose drinking makes you uncomfortable:

- ❤ Meditate on the three Cs of Al-Anon: "I didn't cause it. I can't control it. I can't cure it." Your partner's drinking isn't about you, but it can still affect you. You can't force them to change their behavior, but you can set boundaries around what you'll accept.

- ❤ Journal about how your date's or your partner's drinking makes you feel. Getting those thoughts out of your head can help you process your feelings when or if you talk to them about this.

- ❤ Remember your deal breakers. Are you compromising your deal breakers or your sanity to be with this person? Is your partner's drinking negatively impacting your life or your children's lives?

Making sure that you're safe is essential when navigating these troubling waters. People on the spectrum of AUD may feel judged by your decision not to drink. They may also get agitated or become violent if you decide that you no longer feel safe around them when they're under the influence. Challenging moments like these are reminders of why it's important to build and maintain a safety net. You may want to have a therapist, peer support group, or loved one on call during these difficult conversations.

Checking In

What does liquid courage mean to you? If you feel (or felt) a sense of confidence or increased sexiness while under the influence, write about that feeling. Have you ever felt that way without alcohol? What other activities, people, or foods make you feel similarly confident?

What makes you feel sexy? Perhaps it's visual stimulation (porn, reading erotica). Maybe receiving a compliment from someone you're into makes you feel desired. Or maybe you like to close your eyes and align your mind and body through meditation. Write down what turns you on and why.

Describe your ideal booze-free date. What are you wearing? Who are you with? What are you discussing? What smells are associated with this activity? Are there any food or drinks present? Take time to write down what this date looks like. Or close your eyes and visualize your dream booze-free date.

What presence, whether metaphorical or literal, does/ did alcohol take up in your bed? When was the first time you remember relying on alcohol to help you process difficult emotions? What does emotional intimacy look like in your ideal relationship?

Has your drinking ever been a deal breaker or point of concern for someone else? If so, how did you handle that conversation?

What are your relationship deal breakers? Have they changed since you gave up alcohol or started drinking less?

PART 2

LET'S TALK ABOUT (SOBER) SEX

CHAPTER 6

BIOCHEMISTRY, BOOZE, AND BODIES

E ven if you're not interested in cutting alcohol out of your life entirely, there are strong reasons to leave it out of the bedroom, or at least not make a habit of having drunk sex. I'm not just talking about stuff like self-respect and making good choices for the sake of your mental health—I also mean that, for scientific reasons, sober sex is actually more pleasurable.

If that's true, how come so many people go for drunk sex? The same old thing we've been talking about all along: the security blanket of liquid courage. Alcohol is a mood-altering substance that can create a sense of euphoria. It also lowers inhibitions—and a whole lot of us have inhibitions around sex, for reasons ranging from bad education to active trauma. Alcohol can be a shortcut to feeling emotionally at ease, brave, and free about sex, which is fraught for many people. We gravitate toward alcohol as the accessible, quick, often cheap option for avoiding our hang-ups, instead of channeling our inner bravery to overcome them.

WHAT ALCOHOL DOES TO OUR SEXUAL BODIES

For people with penises, erectile dysfunction and premature ejaculation are common side effects of heavy drinking (heavy here can mean as little as a couple of drinks back to back). Some studies show similar decreased genital response in people with vulvas. Alcohol lowers inhibitions, which may feel subjectively like increased desire—possibly because of our cultural association between alcohol and wild sex! But physiologically, it also reduces blood flow, and blood flow is important to sexual sensitivity. Psychologically, getting drunk may make you feel up for something adventurous in the bedroom, but you may not be up for it physically (pun intended).

Those lowered inhibitions can also lead to lowered standards. This means anything from who you decide to sleep with while intoxicated to whether you decide to use protection. There's a lot to be said for lowered inhibitions, but some inhibitions—such as "I refuse to have sex with someone who won't use a barrier method to prevent STIs"—are essential for your overall health and lifestyle. Facing sexual inhibitions with real courage, rather than liquid courage, allows you to keep your beneficial boundaries in place.

And alcohol affects your whole sex life, not just in the moment. Alcohol is a depressant, which means that consistent over-drinking can hinder brain function, dulling our senses. In layman's terms, booze messes with our ability to feel pleasure (anywhere, not just in bed). This inability to feel pleasure is also known as anhedonia. Symptoms of anhedonia include social withdrawal and losing interest in hobbies or physical intimacy. In other words, drinking may make you feel more uninhibited in the short term, but over time it can dull your interest in everything you normally enjoy, including sex.

SAY WHAT? ANHEDONIA

The inability to feel pleasure or the feeling of being detached from your body.

More sexual bonuses of banging booze-free:

❤ Truly feeling all the physical energy can make you more sexually adventurous than you expected.

❤ Being present can help establish or reinforce intimate trust.

❤ As you gain confidence having sex without alcohol, you learn about exactly what you like and will feel comfortable asking for it.

❤ Deeper emotional connections can enhance the physical experience of having sex.

❤ You'll remember the full experience instead of piecing the patchy night together while hungover the next morning.

What Is Pleasure?

I used to (naively) think that sex was *only* a vagina being penetrated by a penis, seeing any other sexual act as foreplay. (In the predominantly Southern Baptist town where I grew up, even anal sex was considered "not really sex"—at least according to the boys who wanted to pressure you to do it!)

Not only was I wrong, that heteronormative view is one of the many factors that contributed to my sexual dysfunction. That theory invalidated my own sexual experiences with women. I thought sex began with getting into the position the man wanted me to be in, then ended once he climaxed. I never even thought to ask for pleasure of my own—that wasn't what sex was.

I share all of this to encourage you to take a beat and rediscover what sex and pleasure mean to you now—especially if you drank alcohol before your brain was fully developed at age twenty-five. As we grow, our life experiences affect how we process information. It's worth revisiting life lessons from an early age. Do they still check out? Do you still feel that same way? For example, I viewed porn as a manual where now I see it as entertainment. That perspective shift had lasting influence on how I perceive pleasure. Pleasure is anything that brings you feelings of joy or happiness. For some people, especially those on the asexual spectrum, following your pleasure might lead you out of the bedroom entirely. Pleasure can and often does imply sex, but you can also receive pleasure from eating a delicious meal or crushing a deadline.

THE BUILD-UP AND THE LET-DOWN

Alcohol's liquid courage reputation comes from the first part of its biphasic (two-phase) effect on your body and mind. That first phase (one to two drinks) stimulates the brain in a bunch of ways that feel positive, activating pleasure centers and sending dopamine—the brain chemical associated with reward—coursing through the synapses. This stimulation can relax the body and mind, reduce anxiety, and slightly lower inhibitions. But the second phase (multiple drinks or binge drinking) is the opposite; alcohol's depressant properties lead to super-low dopamine levels, making us feel lousy. And over time, it gets harder and harder for our brain to register that initial sense of pleasure. Researchers believe that anhedonia may derive from the brain's broken reward system.

I spoke with neuroscientist Dr. David Briley to learn more about how alcohol's biphasic qualities impact our bodies and minds. The increased confidence from a smaller amount of alcohol, he told me, "is the reason a lot people choose to drink—a lowering of inhibitions, a loosening of the tongue, a warmth as your stress slips away." But increased confidence also means decreased common sense. "Totally sober you might realize that climbing a light pole in sandals is a pretty dumb idea," Dr. Briley said in our conversation. "But with a small loss of inhibition, you might think it could end well. And with a little more disinhibition, you might give it a shot! And with significantly more disinhibition you might lose consciousness on the path to the attempt." The allure of liquid courage is that loss of inhibitions, but remember, you need your inhibitions to stay safe.

The second phase is where alcohol use can get unpleasant—anxiety, depression, eventually even the inability to function emotionally without a drink. But even the first, excitatory phase can be dangerous. "The 'liquid courage' isn't coming from some increased confidence, and certainly not from an increase in capability," Dr. Briley told me. "The 'courage' is simply the effect of increasingly losing the ability to judge what is or isn't an advisable course of action. The degrees may vary, but for most people, alcohol works as a disinhibition from stress, leading to an increase in 'courage.'" This is one of the many reasons it's beneficial to reconnect with yourself, so you can get in touch with your authentic courage that doesn't go away once it's metabolized.

HANGOVER CITY

Of course, alcohol also has an effect on your body outside of your brain. Binge drinking or consuming alcohol in large quantities, in particular, can cause physical body changes during intoxication. Your metabolic system breaks down the ethanol in your drink into an organic compound called acetaldehyde, which creates toxic free radicals (unstable atoms), which in turn . . . make you feel like crap. Our current best guess about the cause of hangovers links symptoms like headaches, bloating, and nausea to high amounts of acetaldehyde in the body. I don't know about you, but feeling bloated and nauseated definitely doesn't get me in the mood.

In short, alcohol messes with every part of our bodies from head to toe, inside and out. It affects how we process foods and process (or don't process) emotions. It can lead to sexual dysfunction as well as emotional arrested development.

I was seventeen the first time I had sex and twenty-nine the first time I had sober sex. That twelve-year time span left me with a lot of emotional and physical baggage to unpack once I embarked on my sober sex journey. Some sober or sober curious folks may want to rip off the proverbial Band-Aid, essentially getting this particular sober first over with, while others may want to wait until they have found a solid connection before getting vulnerable.

SAY WHAT? SOBER FIRSTS

The awkward first time you do something without alcohol (for example: attend a wedding, go on a date, and of course, have sex).

My podcast cohost, Lisa Smith, who first appeared in Chapter 2, went the ripped-Band-Aid route. She traveled from New York City to Park City, Utah, then hooked up with a hot French guy at her friend's wedding. "I was totally attracted to him, but I was scared to have sex without alcohol," she told me. "The bride encouraged me by saying, 'This is perfect! He's hot, plus you never have to see him again!'" The bride's laid-back reminder helped Lisa compartmentalize her first booze-free hookup. "There's an empowerment that comes with being present and sober while having sex. It was an amazing surprise!" she says.

Of course, not all alcohol consumption is created equal. Remember that biphasic quality I talked about earlier? That affects the way alcohol consumption impacts our behavior. When alcohol is consumed mindfully (having one drink), our bodies react differently than when it's consumed heavily (binge drinking). For example: While one glass of wine can have positive feelings that help the drinker relax or get in the mood (phase one), a bottle of wine can go on to cause impotence or vaginal dryness or anhedonia (phase two).

So you don't have to give up alcohol completely to keep it from affecting your sex life—but now that you know a bit more about how alcohol hinders our ability to feel pleasure, you may want to. If so, read on for some alcohol-free alternatives for reducing your inhibitions and accessing your truest sexual self.

CHAPTER 7

ALCOHOL-FREE APHRODISIACS

The most effective way to remove a substance or behavior from your life is to replace it with a healthier alternative. That way, you're not denying yourself anything—you're just changing the specifics. If you're used to using alcohol to get in the mood, then this is a great time to think about booze-free options for getting yourself (and your partner) into a sexy frame of mind. Welcome to the world of aphrodisiacs.

Named after the Greek goddess of love, Aphrodite, aphrodisiacs constitute any substance—from food to certain tree barks to synthetic testosterone—that stimulates sexual desire or excitement or increases sexual pleasure. Some create a physical change in the body and brain, the way a drug does—in fact, many drugs (including, in moderation, alcohol) can be considered aphrodisiacs. We're mostly not going to talk about those, though, because I'm not here to encourage you to replace drinking with ecstasy, amphetamines, or even the hallucinogenic glands of the Bufo toad. Instead, we'll focus on aphrodisiacs that provoke desire through sensory experiences. Think luxurious tastes, sexy smells, titillating textures, and satisfying sounds.

The aphrodisiacs we'll discuss come in several different forms: edible, herbal, and . . . emotional? Let's dig in.

EDIBLE APHRODISIACS

Eating sensual foods with someone that you're into can be a fun, sexy experience—and might even promote blood flow to the genitals (the opposite of what overconsuming alcohol does) by relaxing blood vessels. The feeling of being turned on when you indulge in famously sexy foods is probably at least partly attributable to the placebo effect, but who cares? If a round of oysters followed by chocolate-covered strawberries gets you in the mood without alcohol, order up! The point here is that you're building a genuine connection with someone. If sparks don't fly, at least you're now aware of it instead of getting drunk and letting the night take a different turn. Your clear mind can pick up on that a lot sooner than your mind after happy hour margaritas.

- ❤ Oysters: These shelled creatures are high in zinc, which can boost testosterone and dopamine, which in turn can stimulate sexual desire. Oysters are also high in omega-3 fatty acids which can increase blood flow. Most importantly, they kind of look and feel like . . . well, you know.

- ❤ Chocolate: The cocoa bean has been used as an aphrodisiac since the 1500s. The Mayans, who were big fans of chocolate, associated it with fertility. There's some science behind this too. Chocolate contains tryptophan (which may encourage the brain to release more happy-making neurotransmitters) and phenylethylamine (sometimes known as the love drug due to its mood-boosting, euphoric effects). On a functional level, chocolate's meltability makes for a delectable treat to lick off someone's body. If you're not into chocolate, it's really the licking that matters.

💜 Fruit: Berries are packed with vitamins C and E, stimulating sexual desire. Mango, also known as the love fruit in India, is said to enhance testosterone levels, which can boost sex drive. We all know that vitamins are necessary for a balanced diet. And of course, we feel sexier when we take care of ourselves.

HERBAL APHRODISIACS

My early COVID-19 pandemic hobby, besides crying and doom-scrolling, was studying herbal medicine. I made lots of herbal tinctures to help with sleep and headaches, and even to enhance sex, while learning the history of plant medicines. Who needs liquid courage when you can have herbal courage? Even Mother Nature encourages us to have sober sex by providing us with sexy herbs and plants.

There are several different ways to consume aphrodisiacal herbs. You can steep them like a tea, smoke them, take them sublingually (under the tongue) in tincture form, and inhale them as flower essences—some can even be eaten raw. An herbalist can help you find the right botanical blend, teach you how to properly dose, and show you how to source the ingredients sustainably.

Medicinal plants have been around since long before Western

medicine's "pop a pill for quick effects" approach became the norm. Herbal medicines, similar to SSRIs or a new skincare routine, must be taken regularly before any noticeable physical effects. You're not going to have a cup of ashwagandha tea, then start humping your neighbors. (Or if you do, that says more about you than about the tea. But hey, no judgment here!)

Remember to honor the rich history of Indigenous cultures where these plant medicines are found. And check with your doctor and mental health professionals before experimenting with herbal medicine. Some herbs can negatively interact with existing health conditions and pharmaceutical medications, or lead to forms of dependency. Some of these herbs are illegal in certain states due to their potential euphoric effects. Check your state's laws before purchasing any of the following herbs.

There are dozens of herbal aphrodisiacs, but let's focus on a few.

- ❤ Schisandra berry: This dark red berry is native to northern China. It's said to regulate stress levels, balance hormones, and increase sexual performance. It might even boost semen production or prevent premature ejaculation. Schisandra can also enhance sensory experience (which we'll explore more in a bit). You can find schisandra in powder form or purchase the dried flower from your local herbalist.

- ❤ Ashwagandha: This root, which originated in India and Southeast Asia, may increase sperm production, make it easier to achieve orgasm, and help with erectile dysfunction. Ashwagandha is traditionally used in Ayurveda, but it is also having a moment in the wellness world. Your yoga studio is probably steeping a pot of ashwagandha tea right now, probably more for its purported stress-relieving effects than for sexual reasons (although I don't know your yoga studio). Remember to try and find sustainable sources for this root and other herbal remedies.

- 💜 Damiana: This beautiful yellow flower is native to subtropical environments like Mexico, Texas, and the Caribbean. This ancient aphrodisiac was used by Indigenous cultures long before Spanish colonization. Its Latin name is even *Turnera aphrodisiaca*! Damiana is said to increase sex drive, help with impotence, and stimulate orgasm. Sip damiana tea, smoke an herbal blend with damiana, or try it in tincture form.

- 💜 Cannabis: We all know that weed can get you stoned, but people may not know that there's also evidence cannabis can have some sexual health benefits. Cannabis is known to help people feel relaxed and less anxious, and even to help manage PTSD symptoms (more about these in Chapter 9). Your endocannabinoid system can help your body receive and process this ancient plant medicine. Emotionally, feeling less anxious is obviously going to get you in the mood faster. Physically, studies show that cannabis can help relieve vaginal pain and increase genital response.

SAY WHAT? ENDOCANNABINOID SYSTEM

A cell signaling system within your body that helps regulate metabolism, stress, sleep, fertility, and much more.

If it's too hard to pick just one, you can also try making a cocktail of your favorite herbal aphrodisiacs. (Cocktails don't have to get you drunk! Fruit cocktail, shrimp cocktail, botanical aphrodisiac cocktail . . . you can have plenty of cocktails in your life even without booze.)

Whether or not you believe in herbal medicine, the takeaway here is that these herbs can be a conduit to mindfulness and even a fun form of creativity. That cup of herbal tea may not be an exact replacement for margaritas, but you might feel calm and relaxed while sitting with someone you're into, slowly sipping your personalized herbal blend together. That relaxation alone can create space for solid connection and intimacy that alcohol just can't provide.

EMOTIONAL APHRODISIACS

If herbal medicine isn't for you, maybe you'll appreciate something author and sexologist Gigi Engle refers to as *emotional aphrodisiacs*. "Emotional aphrodisiacs are specific emotional states that trigger desire and arousal, often subconsciously," Engle writes. "Understanding the factors that are specific to you and your sexuality is a big step on the journey to sexual self-discovery, one that has nothing to do with dark chocolate or champagne." Think back to all the work you did in Chapter 1 about dating yourself. That's what Engle's talking about. Discovering what you want, then learning how to communicate it with someone you're into can be a powerful aphrodisiac in and of itself. Rely on the genuine confidence that forms from reconnecting with your intrinsic courage. As Engle puts it: "Alcohol doesn't create confidence; it masks insecurities."

Emotional aphrodisiacs, unlike food and herbs, don't have to be substances. An experience that engages multiple senses can create a sexual experience, according to David Ortmann, a queer and sober psychotherapist and sex therapist and the author of *Sexual Outsiders: Understanding BDSM Sexualities and Communities*.

"The COVID-19 lockdown left us disconnected from our senses, other than visual, because of increased screentime," Ortmann told me. Getting back in touch with the senses is crucial to feeling present. "Put on perfume. Get some sex toys. Taste different types of chocolates and coffees," he said. "Fill your senses with great smells and group bubble baths." Ortmann encourages you to try new things.

Pay attention to how your body and mind react when exposed to different substances or sensual rituals. Maybe the calming smell of lavender reminds you of a romantic vacation. Or a song reminds you of a time when you and your beloved saw the artist in concert? Perhaps the velvety texture of whipped cream feels playful on your fingers. Or the spiciness of your dinner gives you an adrenaline rush. Remember that alcohol overuse can dull our senses, so indulging in sensory experiences may be a new, possibly overwhelming feeling. Give yourself space to approach these experiences at a pace that feels right for you.

GET SEXY WITH BOOZE-FREE DRINKS

Chris Marshall is a pioneer in the nonalcoholic drink scene. In 2017 he opened Sans Bar in Austin, Texas, one of the very first brick-and-mortar sober bars. He also travels the country hosting sober bar pop-ups. His most recent endeavor, Sans Bar Academy, teaches the wonderful world of booze-free mixology through Zoom courses. So naturally, he's the first person I went to when I wanted to learn more about how to incorporate mocktails into sober sex and dating. "Alcohol-free drinks are an invitation to be deliciously divergent from everything we've been conditioned to believe about connection to other people. When we are making alcohol-free drinks we have the freedom to play with flavors that set the mood for deeper connection," he told me. "While taste can be subjective, there's something wildly hot about preparing something for a romantic interest, especially if it is served in a cute little coupe glass." Just like the aphrodisiacs I mentioned earlier, it doesn't matter if a sexy nonalcoholic drink "works." What matters is how each of you feel and the effort of creativity put into these experiences.

Marshall also suggests involving sensory deprivation, such as blindfolds, and sensory play into your drink tasting. "Carefully guide the glass to your partner's nose and allow them to take in your creation slowly. Ask about the notes that meet their nose. Can they hear the fizz of seltzers? What flavors do they notice first? Can they guess which ingredients are in the drink?" These experiences offer fun, unique bonding moments and trust building.

If you're having a hard time believing that the nonalcoholic drink scene is thriving, here's a little more info. In 2021, Business Insider reported that sales of no-booze drinks had grown by 33 percent over the year. Heineken brought in $54 million in sales in 2020 from its alcohol-free beer alone, and nonalcoholic Athletic Brewing was the top-selling beer brand at Whole Foods in 2022. And Budweiser Zero sponsored the 2021 Super Bowl. Booze-free bottle shops and bars are popping up all across the world, and not just in big-city areas. Many restaurants now offer interesting nonalcoholic drink options or full mocktail menus. Gone are the days of O'Doul's and watery Near Beer. We now have dealcoholized rosé, CBD seltzer, and bottled botanicals. So yes, now is the perfect time to incorporate booze-free drinks into your pre-sex rituals.

Sexy Drink Garnishes

I asked nonalcoholic mixologist extraordinaire Chris Marshall to suggest a few sexy garnishes to level up your zero-proof drink game. Here's what he recommended:

- **Cotton candy:** There's something undeniably playful about cotton candy. Super sweet garnishes like cotton candy pair very well with more tart profiles. Think sours, shrubs, and tonic-based drinks.

- **Ice spheres:** Beyond the sleek aesthetic of a clear globe floating in a glass, the smooth texture of an ice sphere makes it versatile as both a way to chill your drink and a way to heat up an after-drinks foreplay sesh.

- **Stemmed cherries:** I think this one is pretty obvious. After you have enjoyed the fruit, take turns watching each other attempt to tie the cherry stem with your mouth.

- **Leather:** Not actual leather, but fruit leather. Using a long ribbon of fruit leather, line your glass with this edible naughtiness to add a little spice and sweetness at the same time.

Something that all these aphrodisiac types have in common is their emphasis on slowing down to get present, perhaps the polar opposite of liquid courage. Alcohol-fueled arousal can give you a sense of urgency—you want to get it on *now now now*, before you lose your enhanced nerve (and before the booze makes you dry and/or flaccid)! And there's definitely something hot about urgency, but being present in your body is sexy too. As you learn to appreciate sober sex, you'll find that slow doesn't have to mean boring. It doesn't even have to mean moving at a glacial pace! The point of slowing down is not to become physically less active, but to connect mentally with what you're doing, at any speed.

CHAPTER 8

SEXUAL LIBERATION WITHOUT BOOZE

You may be worrying that without liquid courage, you won't be able to have liberated, uninhibited sex. But actually, booze-free sex will help you get more authentically in touch with your wild side—especially if most of your previous sexual exploration has been under the influence of alcohol! Now is your chance not only to learn more about what you like, but to learn specifically about what *sober* you likes, and what it feels like to approach sexual liberation with real courage.

Sexual liberation can mean anything from exploring kink to coming to terms with your sexuality or gender identity to . . . embracing the fact that you love vanilla sex. You don't have to be outside the mainstream to be liberated, as long as you're getting in touch with your genuine desires! The point is to free yourself from the societal expectations of what sex *should* be. It's time to discover what you like and realize you don't need alcohol to tap into your sexual self.

My sexual liberation is inextricably linked to my sobriety. Once I stopped comparing my relationship with alcohol to other people's relationships with alcohol, I could finally see how damaging my drinking habits were. Embracing sexuality can be similar—when you stop worrying about what everyone else is doing, you can tap into what feels right for you.

Mei McIntosh, a Seattle-based sober DJ and founder of the online community The Creative Sober, says giving up alcohol helped them feel more sexually liberated. "I've explored the deepest parts of my sexuality and the different dynamics of relationships, from polyamory to monogamy," they told me. "I've also embraced gender fluidity that I would have never discovered if I didn't quit alcohol. I think what happened is that when I put down the drink, I began to feel what was happening inside me and started finding honest answers from curiosity." I had a similar eye-opening experience when embracing my bisexuality once I quit drinking.

People like McIntosh and me benefit from significant advances in the way popular culture portrays sexuality and gender. Shows like *Sex and the City* and *The L Word*, once at the forefront of sexual liberation, didn't fully embrace the bi and trans communities. In one episode of *Sex and the City*, for instance, Carrie told viewers that bisexuality is a phase and that she couldn't date a bisexual man because she's "too old for games." The reboots for both shows, *The L Word: Generation Q* in 2019 and *And Just Like That* in 2022, now have diverse representations of the colorful LGBTQIA+ rainbow. (Both shows also have storylines about alcohol abuse.) There is now also accurate bi/pan and trans representation in shows like *The Bold Type*, *Euphoria*, *Schitt's Creek*, *Pose*, and *Crazy Ex-Girlfriend*. (The last of these shows even offers a killer bisexual anthem called

"Gettin' Bi.")

Nuanced bisexual representation in culture eclipsed the imposter syndrome that told me I wasn't "bi enough." To me, bisexuality means experiencing attraction to all genders regardless of my relationship status, sexual history, or sexual future. I don't need to validate my sexuality like a parking ticket—and I don't need to drink alcohol to get in touch with it.

But regardless of improvements on screen, I could never have achieved this level of honesty, awareness, and self-love if I still drank. Before I quit drinking, I frequently googled "Do I have a drinking problem?" I now know that anyone researching that question could probably benefit from at least a dry month or two. Discovering my bisexuality was very similar for me. I spent so much time googling "Am I bisexual?" that I now can only look back and laugh. I wish I could shout back through time to my past self, "You definitely have a drinking problem and you're definitely bisexual!"

While my sexual liberation helped me stop artificially limiting my sexual attraction, some people realize they feel liberated admitting that they don't experience sexual attraction at all. I spoke with several asexual people who mentioned that they used alcohol to make themselves enjoy or feel interested in sex. "After I stopped drinking, I noticed how uncomfortable sex was for me all the time," Jess Schilling, a sober asexual person that I met through Twitter, told me. "I had felt like something was not quite heterosexual about me for a long time, it just required the sober clarity to get to the why of it. But on reflection, I absolutely did use alcohol in all of my sexual relationships to tolerate partnered sex." Though I'm allosexual, I relate to Schilling's experience. I also used alcohol to alter my sexual experiences.

Maybe you think you might be part of the LGBTQIA+ community but never explored that side of yourself. Or maybe you only let yourself embrace your potential queerness after a few drinks. Reevaluating your relationship with alcohol is also a great time to learn about all of the beautiful colors of our rainbow, and think about whether any of them apply to you. And remember that the Q stands for *questioning* for moments just like these.

I'm a nerd with an insatiable appetite to learn all of the things, so yes, I suggest utilizing the opportunities of the information age to help discover your sexuality or gender identity. There's a vast number of free resources just a click away. Here are a few ways to dip your toe into the rainbow:

- ❤ Follow #queerandsober or #gayandsober on social media.

- ❤ Find a sober or sober curious queer meetup group. This sounds more niche than it is. Social media and meetup apps have a corner for everyone. You may like connecting with people like you, whether you read Reddit threads or attend an in-person hangout.

- ❤ Make a list of sexual curiosities, then google away! Learn more about what piques your interest through podcasts, essays, books, or social media. Remember that your sexual interests are valid as long as everyone involved is an enthusiastically consenting adult.

- ❤ Watch queer porn or read queer erotica. Lucie Blush and Erika Lust are ethical adult filmmakers who make porn you've probably never seen before. More into erotica? Find titillating stories online by searching for "erotica" and your particular interests, or check your app store for audio-based options if you'd rather listen to sexy stories.

GET HONEST ABOUT ORGASMS

The honesty that helped me ditch alcohol also helped me stop faking orgasms, a habit I developed in my late teen years and broke when I stopped drinking. I read *Faking It: The Lies Women Tell About Sex and the Truths They Reveal* by Lux Alptraum in early sobriety. Reading about other women and nonbinary people who fake orgasms for various reasons helped me feel less alone, which at first felt comforting. Then that comfort turned into disappointment, as I realized so many others aren't advocating for their pleasure. "Why do women fake orgasms?" Alptraum writes. "Perhaps because we prioritize our ideas about what pleasure looks like over actual pleasure itself. Sometimes faking an orgasm is just a way of closing the gap between expectation and reality." That's precisely what it was for me. I thought I was weird for not climaxing when a penis entered me like people did in movies or porn. So I faked to appear normal.

I stopped faking orgasms the first time I had semi-sober sex. His name was Aleksander, and he was a Polish guy who moved to New York City for the same reason we all did: to follow a dream. But before we had sober sex, we had a drunken hookup. We had met at a bar a few weeks earlier through mutual friends. We bonded over those mutual friends and a shared love of Nirvana. Back then, I thought someone was my soulmate if we liked the same music. I went home with Aleksander a few hours later. We drank, smoked pot, and made out before I enjoyed my buzzed walk home.

A few weeks later, we hung out at his place again. He tossed me a Coors Light. In the weeks between our drunken hookup and the moment he handed me that beer, something had shifted in me. I'd begun evaluating my relationship with alcohol, questioning why I drank, what alcohol gave me, and what it took from me. One sip of that mediocre light beer from that shiny silver can made me realize I didn't want it. So I set it aside.

We kissed and eventually ended up in bed. "I've never had an orgasm with someone else. Only when I'm alone," I told him. That was the first time I said that to someone. I felt exposed for announcing my perceived flaw out loud. For loving sex even though I couldn't climax from it. For being so vulnerable with someone I barely knew. He appeared unfazed, unaware that my confession was a moment of revelatory growth. "Well, you haven't slept with me yet," he joked. This playfully arrogant response popped up with other partners after Aleksander, as if their skills were powerful enough to reverse a lifetime of anxiety and trauma.

Being this honest with someone was much scarier than reprising my comfortable performance role as Woman Who Climaxes. He was kind. He put on records that he knew I liked. While Alanis was telling us that we oughta know, he went down on me. I was too in my head to enjoy getting head. *You're a freak. You'll never have an orgasm—especially not with this guy. Just give up.* He sensed my tension. "Relax and let me lick you," he said. I laughed, and it did calm me down. I didn't have an orgasm, but something more climactic was on the horizon.

I stopped drinking the following day.

SOME OF THE WILDEST SEX IS ALREADY SOBER

The sex column that assigned me the mirror masturbation article from Chapter 1 also gave me several pieces about sex work. I've watched porn since high school, but researching those articles opened my eyes to how ignorant I was of the world of the adult film industry. I naively assumed that because I used alcohol to feel more confident in bed, people who have sex for a living must also use substances in the same way. I was shocked to learn drugs and alcohol are often frowned upon at sex parties and on adult film sets. This discovery led to me interviewing dozens of sober sex workers and learning that some of today's top adult performers feel empowered in their booze-free lives.

I spoke with Leya Tanit, a former sex worker and the founder of Pineapple Support, a mental health nonprofit for sex workers, to learn more about the role alcohol plays (or doesn't!) on an adult film set. "Consent is a hot topic in the adult industry. Before going into any production, each performer has a consent checklist (a yes and no list). And people can change this at any moment during the shoot or the day of. There's no drinking on set at all," she told me. "If someone turns up drunk, they're not allowed to take part and the set is shut down for the day. If someone has been drinking, the sex is not consensual. Plus you get a better performer when someone has a clear mind. No one wants to see a glassy-eyed adult performer."

The same approach goes for sex and play parties. I assumed that people needed to be wasted to experiment with kink or public sex. Man, was I wrong! Most ethical sex parties actually have a drink *maximum* or encourage no alcohol due to the importance of being fully present in your mind and body before consenting to sex. I chatted with arguably the kinkiest person on the internet and the author of *Boyslut: A Memoir and Manifesto*, Zachary Zane, about how consent and alcohol connect at these fuck fiestas. "Drinking is typically discouraged at sex parties," he told me. "When you're drunk, you not only cannot give consent, but you're also less likely to pick up any nonverbal cues when flirting with someone. Not to mention that it is dangerous to engage in BDSM sex when one person is inebriated. So, unexpectedly, sex parties are some of the most welcoming places for folks who are sober!" Unexpected is right! It turns out my bacchanalian theory was wrong. Those not-so-underground orgies and dominatrix dungeons are filled with intrinsic courage, not liquid courage.

Get into Toys
(And Possibly Vice Versa)

Sometimes when I recommend that sober or sober curious folks incorporate sex toys into the bedroom, people tell me that they don't need a sex toy. Maybe not, but they're called toys for a reason—they're *fun*! I also think of sex toys as wellness tools. Vibrators and sex swings and handcuffs add some extra flair to your sex life (and might make orgasm more achievable), but did you know there are also gadgets that actually make sex more accessible? There are pillows that make certain positions possible or easier (especially for people with nonnormative bodies), and which can make those hard-to-reach places a bit more attainable. There are tools to strengthen your pelvic floor, which can make sex more pleasurable for people with vaginas. For folks with large penises, there are buffer rings that help make penetration less painful for a partner. And of course there's lube. So many types of lube. Everyone, please buy some lube.

I talked to Rebecca Alvarez Story, a sexologist and cofounder of Bloomi Wellness, for advice on stocking your goody drawer with the basics.

- ❣ Grab some pleasure oils. There are so many options these days! Whether you need a libido boost or want to increase sensitivity, learn about the beautiful world of pleasure oils.

- ❣ Try body massage. Some folks may not think of massage as sexual or sensual, but it can be. Whether you're single or in a relationship, massaging our bodies can help us relax and get in the mood without alcohol.

- Opt for multipurpose toys. Want more bang for your buck? Check out toys with more than one feature like double-sided dildos, vibrators with multiple vibration patterns, or devices that can be used on numerous body parts (such as ones that offer vaginal and clitoral stimulation).

- Stick with medical-grade silicone. This type of silicone prevents infection while feeling silky smooth to the touch. Remember to always, always, always wash your toys!

At the risk of sounding like a PG-13 after-school special, the best sex toy is communication—especially for newly sober or sober curious folks still finding their footing.

FOREPLAY AND AFTERCARE

Rethinking sex in sobriety helped me redefine foreplay. I always thought of oral sex as a standard appetizer to prepare me for the main course. While giving or receiving oral sex absolutely can be a fun pre-intercourse ritual, it's also a delicious snack on its own. Foreplay can also be a conversation. "I would never have thought that talking could turn me on," Katie Mack, a sober actor and Webby-award-winning creator of the *F*cking Sober* podcast, shared with me. "Talking about my day with someone I'm into, then hearing about their day, reminds me that we're both just humans looking for connection." This might seem obvious to someone accustomed to alcohol-free sex, but this discovery is revelatory to people like Mack and me. Looking back, I see that I actively avoided serious conversations with sexual partners when I drank to avoid intimacy. Now I look forward to having sincere conversations with Nick to solidify our emotional bond.

The term *aftercare* is popular in the BDSM and kink communities as well as in instructions about caring for a new tattoo or piercing, but you don't need whips and chains (or fresh ink!) to have a mindful discussion about the sex you just had with your partner(s).

SAY WHAT? AFTERCARE

Originally from the kink world, this term refers to a post-encounter check-in where each party expresses how they feel about the experience, both physically and emotionally. The term can also be generalized to similar check-ins after sex, which serve as a grounding technique after trying something new or revisiting a familiar position.

Sample aftercare discussions:

❤ I loved when you _____. It made me feel _____. (Humans love compliments, especially about something as vulnerable as sex. Give your partner a gold star and they'll probably try to earn another one!)

❤ What did you think of that new move? I read about it online and wanted to try it out.

❤ What was your favorite part about _____?

❤ I wasn't as into _____. Maybe we can try _____ next time?

❤ Next time, can you _____? I like it because _____.

ASK FOR WHAT YOU WANT

Asking for what you want in bed is also a great way to filter out folks who don't deserve access to your body and mind. If a sexual partner doesn't want to please you, send them on their way. They're just in bed with you to get what they want. You're not responsible for anyone else's orgasm—unless, of course, that's part of a fun, consensual game you're playing.

Maybe you've only spoken up in bed after a few drinks. Maybe you've never advocated for your own pleasure. Either way, here are some tips on how to get the conversation started. Whoever you're sleeping with is lucky as hell. They should want to know what pleases you!

Some sample conversation beginners:

- ❤ "I'd love to show you what turns me on." Then demonstrate with your hand before guiding their hand over yours until you both feel comfortable letting them take over.

- ❤ When you want to try something new but have no idea where to start: "I'd love to mix things up—is there anything new you'd like to try?"

- ❤ When you want to try something that you saw or read about elsewhere: "A sex educator I follow on TikTok recommended this position. I'd love to try this with you! May I show you?"

- ❤ When they touch you somewhere you don't want to be touched: "I actually don't like to be touched there, but I love when you touch me here." Then slowly move their hand.

- ❤ When you want to incorporate some toys: "I got us a present. Can we bring it to bed tonight?"

- ❤ When you thought you were ready, but you need more time: "I'm actually not in the right headspace. Can we _____ instead?"

GO ON A SENSE JOURNEY

You might think that alcohol turns your libido up to eleven, but as we discussed in Chapter 6 excessive booze actually turns down your pleasure centers. Sober sex can bring more intense physical and emotional sensations, which can feel overwhelmingly new and scary. I drank because I wanted sameness, so the newness of sober sex took some getting used to. If boozy sex is like painting in the dark, sober sex is like finally being able to see your paints and paintbrush again. And buying an easel. And experimenting with lots of fun color palettes.

This newfound sensory experience can feel overstimulating to anyone in early sobriety or sober curiosity, especially neurodivergent folks with sensory sensitivities. Think about going out to eat at a restaurant. All of your senses are fully engaged: your eyes look at the menu and the people around you. Your ears hear the server, the background music, and the discussion at the next table over. The chair you're sitting in provides physical sensations, just like the clothes on your body. You smell the lemon in your water, the saffron in your soup, and the salmon your date ordered. Then you eat, tasting each bite while your other four senses are also on high alert. That's a lot to process, right? Even more so for anyone with disordered eating habits or body image issues.

The same experience can happen in bed when you're trying sober sex for the first time. Your eyes watch your partner(s) as they lean in for a kiss, slowly working their way down your neck. Your ears process the sound of them telling you how much you turn them on. Goosebumps arise as your skin reacts to their facial hair or the softness of their lips. You taste the saltiness of their sweat while their pheromones intoxicate you. A simple dinner date or being fully present for a sexual experience can quite literally make you catch feelings. Of course, you may not experience all five senses, but you may still experience the same kinds of sensory overload.

Before you engage in booze-free sex, let's explore some ways to feel comfortably connected with your senses. The following tips can help you stay mindful while working toward a physical goal of enjoying booze-free sex. Of course, different people have different sensoria, so adapt this however makes sense for you and your partner or partners! If one of you is deaf or hard of hearing, for instance, you may (or may not!) want to skip sound-based sense play, and if one of you has sensory integration issues you may want to take everything more slowly.

Step One: Reconnect with Your Senses

Since we can't selectively numb physical sensations, at least not without local anesthetic, alcohol swoops in to numb them all. This means that if you've always been drunk—or even just buzzed—during sex, you may never have experienced maximum pleasure. Take time to reconnect with your body and mind through some sensory play. You can do this sensory exploration solo, with a friend or therapist, or with one or more partners. Think of the following exercises as training wheels. Start slow, then build up slowly. Try your best to observe your sensual experiences without assigning value or passing judgment. Here are a few ways to reconnect with various senses before engaging in sober sex:

- ❤ Listen to music intentionally. Which instruments do you hear? What are the musical vibrations? How does the song make you feel?

- ❤ Gently run your fingernails down your arm or rub velvet against your cheek. Playing with different textures can stimulate your nerves in ways you've never experienced. How does your skin react to different fabrics?

- ❤ Practice mindful eating. This can mean eating silently (no Netflix!), putting your fork down between bites, or even closing your eyes while eating. The point here is to focus on the food. Notice the textures. Inhale the smells. Identify the seasonings and spices.

- Sit in your apartment while wearing noise-cancelling headphones or earplugs or while listening to ambient sounds pumping through your earbuds. What do you notice about your own home without the hum of the dishwasher or with your dog's barking muffled?

- Sports medicine doctors say injured athletes can train while in bed by simply visualizing. Why not try visualizing your ideal, alcohol-free sexual encounter! Is there a date beforehand? If so, what are you doing? What are each of you wearing? Who makes the first move?

Step Two:
Embrace More Intense Sensations

When you want to remove the training wheels, the next step is sensory deprivation. For example, when focusing on taste, try closing your eyes. To focus on visual senses, throw in some earplugs. Sensory deprivation simply means reducing sensory experiences so you can focus on a few or just one at a time.

Sensory deprivation is why some people enjoy being blindfolded in bed. Closing your eyes or having them covered increases the awareness of your other senses. Sensory deprivation might sound extreme, but that's what many of us do subconsciously with alcohol. When you drink to reduce pre-date jitters or bedroom anxiety, you're also depriving yourself of a full sensory experience.

The following exercises build on step one:

- Now that you feel comfortable listening to music intentionally, try it with your eyes closed. Perhaps you go into a meditative state while lying on your bed. Or maybe you internally visualize yourself acting out the lyrics in the song.

- Go for a walk or sit outside while wearing noise-canceling head-phones or earplugs. What does outside look like without the sound of the jackhammers or children running around?

- Close your eyes or wear a blindfold while you take a bite of your food. I once attended a blindfolded dinner. Each bite, flavor, aroma, and texture offered a unique dining experience, allowing me to taste food in a whole new way.

- Leave the blindfold or noise-canceling headphones on, then revisit the texture play from step one. How does that velvet feel on your cheek with your eyes or ears covered? Do you prefer the sensation one way or the other?

- If your sober sex visualization from step one turns you on, why not take matters into your own hands?

Step Three: Go from Sensual to Sexual

Now it's time to have kickass sober sex. Or at the very least, enjoy-able sex while being fully engaged instead of buzzed or inebriated.

- Listen to music or high frequency tones that relax you before getting it on. Don't think of it as background music. Pay attention to the music and lyrics. Your partner(s) can join, too!

- Look your partner in the eye right before going in for a kiss. It doesn't have to be a long, awkward stare down. Just a simple gaze that lasts a tad longer than usual might make you feel some excitement in your belly—or other places!

- Ask your partner(s) if they want to try texture play with you. They may not understand what this means, so create a sexy show and tell moment.

💜 Recreate that sensual fantasy that you visualized. Of course, we all know that fantasy is vastly different from reality, but there's no harm in getting creative while making sure you feel comfortable! Remember, sex is supposed to be a fun activity that physically, and sometimes emotionally, connects you to someone else. You can (and should) stop or take a break if you begin to feel uncomfortable.

This sensory play can help you gauge your sober sex comfort levels. If a hot and heavy makeout sesh with lots of skin contact feels overwhelming to your senses, that might be your body telling you that you're not ready to take it any further. Comfort is a prerequisite to having good, consensual sober sex.

While sober me still has a rapidly expanding drawer of sex toys (I *am* a sex writer), I'm happy to admit I prefer old-fashioned missionary with eye contact. Drunk me thought I needed all the bells and whistles to feel empowered in bed, mostly because I was more concerned with pleasing someone else than figuring out what I wanted. Replacing liquid courage with intrinsic courage taught me that holding hands and making eye contact requires more vulnerability than having a threesome or using sex toys. I finally replaced the performative element with asking for what I wanted.

CHAPTER 9

HANDLING TRAUMA AND PTSD

Over 400,000 people experience sexual violence every year in the US, and many of us cope with that trauma using alcohol. If it's historically taken a little liquid courage to get you through a sexual encounter without bad feelings, sober sex might present a significant hurdle. There's a lot of shame, guilt, and various uncomfortable emotions that come along with reckoning with our pasts. It's difficult to feel empowered in bed if the bedroom is a source of trauma—and it's really hard to put away the security blanket that has let you bypass or ignore that trauma for a while.

My way of coping with PTSD (before my official diagnosis) was to leave my body and mind, outsourcing those repressed emotions to alcohol. I kept feelings at bay by treating sex as a performance (as I mentioned in Chapter 1), and always, always being drunk. It was freaking exhausting, but I didn't know any other way. Some people with sexual trauma go in another direction, avoiding sex entirely because the experience dredges up so many bad feelings. (Some even consider this their sexual orientation; a minority of people on the asexual spectrum identify as caedosexual, meaning that they no longer feel sexual attraction due to trauma.)

A yoga teacher once told me that our bodies feel anxiety and excitement in the same way: Heart beating out of our chests. Fidgeting in our seats. Tense muscles. It's actually up to our minds to assign value to those bodily responses based on past experiences, deciding how to feel about those physical responses. Is feeling less anxious about sober sex as easy as a quick shift in perspective? It sure can be. "Physical arousal is a sympathetic nervous system response. And guess what else is? Trauma response," Dr. Wood, the sex therapist from Chapter 3, told me. "Alcohol turns off the prefrontal cortex, switches off hypervigilance, and allows the body to experience the very same symptoms that would otherwise be read as fear and anxiety." In other words, a traumatized brain might interpret any physical excitation—including sexual arousal—as fear. Alcohol helps you shut off that part of the brain.

While I don't identify as caedosexual, sex has changed since certain things happened to me while I was drunk, and changed again as I processed them in sobriety. I had to learn how to trust myself and trust others. Much of this practice came from nurturing my comfort zone.

NURTURE YOUR COMFORT ZONE

Capitalism, self-help gurus, and #girlboss culture preach the gospel of getting outside of your comfort zone to make a significant change or grow as a person. While I believe that there's a place and time for this type of prescriptive advice, it's not one-size-fits-all. Encouraging people to leave their comfort zone can actually be harmful to folks with mental health issues, especially those with PTSD navigating sober sex and dating. My hot take? Growth happens *inside* your comfort zone.

Comfort zones get such a bad rap that when you hear the term, you might assume some toxic positivity BS is sure to follow or that someone is trying to disguise bullying as life coaching. But getting in touch with what makes you feel safe is a key part of reconnecting with your intrinsic courage—and for people with sexual trauma, that feeling of safety is especially crucial and hard to come by. "Asking someone with PTSD to feel comfortable in the bedroom is like asking somebody to put their hands back on the stove that just burned them," Dr. Wood told me. "People who've experienced sexual trauma often feel betrayed not only by others or a world that traumatized them, but by their very own body. It requires permission that this body is worthy of understanding, that it's valued for the information it carries that is coded in anxiety, panic, dissociation, vigilance, anger, shame."

I had to learn how to cultivate and nurture my comfort zone to live, let alone thrive. This meant years of therapy, processing my past to live a healthier present and future. I had to learn how to trust people before letting them in, figuratively and literally. I also had to unlearn the internalized societal narrative that sex is something done to women as opposed to something we can also seek pleasure from.

This much-needed unlearning taught me that I need to feel safe with someone else before I can genuinely feel comfortable getting sexual with them. I'm proof that growth can also happen while staying inside our comfort zones. And that comfort doesn't need to incorporate booze.

I explored this topic with my therapist, Lynn Macarin-Mara, who shared tips on trauma bonding in Chapter 2. Together, we came up with some tools to identify and nurture your comfort zone so you can be fully present for alcohol-free sex and dating.

- ❤ What does your existing comfort zone look like or feel like? Is this space literal or metaphorical? What might make it even cozier?

- ❤ What does safety mean to you? Who do you know that makes you feel safe? Who do you know that makes you feel *unsafe*? Discerning between the two might give you a home base to revisit when dating and sex feel overwhelming without alcohol.

- ❤ Create ways to access this comfort zone while you're on a date. If your newly decorated closet makes you feel at ease, keep a piece of the wallpaper in your wallet! Does snuggling with your fur baby give you all the good feels? Make your phone's lock screen a photo of your pet to glance at throughout the date.

- ❤ Talk to someone you trust (friend, therapist, sponsor) about what makes you feel safe and comfortable. Saying these words out loud can help boost your confidence because you're proudly advocating for yourself!

- ❤ Remember all the work you did on dating yourself in Chapter 1? Revisit the prompts and exercises that helped you feel empowered and safe.

MANAGING THE SYMPTOMS

So what's next? Let's say you've done the therapy, talking, crying, and processing. Now it's time to have some fun between the sheets without getting three sheets to the wind. I spoke to Keegan Herring, a queer mindfulness-based therapist, about how people with PTSD can feel safe while having sex in early sobriety or sober curiosity. He shared some helpful, proactive tips as well as some tips for in the moment.

Proactive tips:

❤ Create goals related to safe, booze-free sex, then communicate them with your partner(s).

❤ Identify a safe word (and a meaning for that word!) that you and your partner feel comfortable with. (Try something like: "When I say 'avocado,' that means I want to stop having sex and just snuggle for a bit.")

❤ Share your comfort zone list with your partner(s). This type of communication can help build mindful, meaningful relationships—and great sex!

In the moment:

❤ Let your partner(s) know what's happening. You can say something like, "It's not personal, this is just something I'm going through."

❤ Take space to try a grounding exercise like breath work or identifying five objects in the room to remind you where you are physically.

❤ Repeat a mantra, such as "everything is OK" or "I'm safe right now in this moment."

CAN CANNABIS HELP?

In Chapter 7, we talked about the aphrodisiac perks of some herbal medicines, including cannabis. In addition to helping reduce genital discomfort and stimulate libido, cannabis in particular is often used to manage PTSD symptoms. Some people who avoid alcohol altogether may still enjoy the medicinal or recreational benefits of cannabis; these people sometimes describe themselves as "California sober." You don't want to thoughtlessly replace alcohol with weed, and some people who are reevaluating their drinking behavior will want to avoid all mind-altering substances altogether. But if you're comfortable with non-booze substance use, cannabis can be a healthy alternative for folks with PTSD transitioning into alcohol-free sex and dating.

SAY WHAT? CALIFORNIA SOBER

Abstaining from alcohol but still mindfully consuming cannabis or psychedelics.

Sophie St. Thomas, the author of *Finding Your Higher Self* and *Weed Witch*, celebrates weed's myriad health benefits. "I was completely sober for two years, and then I started using cannabis medicinally for PTSD from being raped," she shared with me. "Cannabis lets me relax and eventually find joy in sex again." The relaxation she mentions isn't just a state of mind; it's science. Remember the endocannabinoid system discussed in Chapter 7? Your body produces its own cannabinoids, which serve a number of roles, including regulating emotion and helping the brain let go of learned trauma responses. External cannabinoids, used responsibly, can have similar effects.

Dr. June Chin, a physician who specializes in cannabis, explained to me how traumatized minds react to alcohol and cannabis differently. "Trauma survivors have been found to have problems with neurotransmitter signaling of serotonin and glutamate. These neurotransmitters correlate with the fight-or-flight response," she said in an email interview. "Where alcohol can deplete the brain's production of neurotransmitters like GABA (gamma-aminobutyric acid that blocks nerve signals like anxiety and fear from reaching the brain) and glutamate (aids in memory and brain function), cannabis can have the opposite effect since it's a GABA uptake inhibitor—it creates a surplus of GABA in the brain, which creates the quieting and calming effect. Patients report medical cannabis working to 'take the edge off' and 'turn the volume down' on anxiety." Which is a fancy way of saying that weed can possibly help folks reconnect with pleasure while on their booze-free journey.

Cannabis is still illegal in a number of US states, and illegal outside of prescribed medical use in many more. Make sure you know the legal status of weed in your area before you use it. There's also ongoing debate about whether the benefits of cannabis outweigh the downsides of using mind-altering substances, and ultimately nobody can make that decision for you. Don't swap out alcohol for weed if you have reason to believe that weed will have an equally negative influence on your life! That said, it's also worth thinking in terms of harm reduction. Harm reduction might not make sense to anyone who's never experienced trauma or substance misuse. But for a trauma survivor trying to find joy in sex after a devastating life experience, replacing alcohol with cannabis, even temporarily, can offer long-term positive effects.

SAY WHAT? HARM REDUCTION

A growing movement of public health policies designed to decrease the negative consequences of drug use without enforcing abstinence. Examples: needle exchange programs, supervised injection sites, and replacing harder drugs like opioids or alcohol with plant medicines like cannabis or psychedelics.

Checking In

How has alcohol's biphasic effect impacted you when on a date or getting intimate? Write down how you've felt after one drink and after several.

Are there any herbs, foods, or nonalcoholic drinks that make you feel sexy? Write down each one, then describe how you feel during or after consuming it.

What does sexual liberation mean to you?

What role does or did alcohol play in your sexuality?

Do the sexual activities you prefer change when you're drinking versus when you're not drinking?

If you've experienced trauma, how does/did alcohol play a role in managing the discomfort of PTSD?

What does your comfort zone look like, and how can you help yourself get there?

PART 3

UNDRUNK LOVE

CHAPTER 10

CONSCIOUS COUPLING

In the same way that I had to step back and reevaluate my relationship with alcohol, I also had to step back and evaluate my relationship with *relationships*. Remember your work on getting to know yourself without alcohol in the first few chapters? This is where it all comes together. Now that you know the value of dating yourself, how to have awesome sex without booze, and where to have fun, sober dates, let's finally explore what it's like to be in a conscious, loving relationship that doesn't center around cocktails.

For me, being in a sober relationship is the polar opposite of being in a drunk or buzzed relationship, mostly because I'm my genuine self without alcohol. Nick and I are *far* from perfect, but we both value communication as the most important aspect of our relationship, which means that we're usually on the same page. And when we're not, well, we talk about it.

Just because you're no longer dating and you found your true love (or true loves) doesn't mean the work ends; this is where the real work begins. I had to identify, then unlearn, my drunken toxic relationship habits in therapy (jealousy, insecurity, projecting childhood trauma, unrealistic expectations) before I could be a good partner in sobriety.

That alone time you spent in early sobriety or sober curiosity hopefully connected you with your intrinsic courage. Here are a few ways to channel your newfound courage while in a committed relationship instead of opening a bottle of wine:

💜 Speak up for what you want and don't want, whether it's deciding where to go for dinner or debating trying that new thing in bed. Being fully present with your emotions can prevent you from doing something that you truly don't want to do. There's a difference between being open to compromise and being a people pleaser. Sticking to your intrinsic courage can prevent you from the latter.

💜 Be discerning. That list of deal breakers doesn't go out the window just because they put a ring on it. The more comfortable you get in a relationship, the more old habits tend to slip in. Leaving beer goggles out of the relationship can make you aware of what's happening and how you're treated.

💜 Acknowledge what's changed. If you're reevaluating your relationship with alcohol and your partner isn't, they may feel unsettled or overwhelmed by changes to your preferences or behaviors. You may react to things in a different way than they're used to, or express dislike of things you used to tolerate. You may be more emotional, or less. Acknowledging and talking openly about it will help. A simple "this might be weird for you, and trust me, it's weird for me too" will go a long way.

To learn more about long-term, alcohol-free relationships, I interviewed Ralph Homan, a seventy-two-year-old author and retired financial services entrepreneur with thirty-seven years of sobriety (my entire lifetime!). "Communication starts with mentation," he told me—in other words, with using your mind. "Mentation, thus communication, is so much better when sober," he went on. "Other personality issues may still get in the way but at least impaired judgment and bad temper from being drunk won't be among them." I appreciate how Ralph mentions other personality issues because, as we've discussed in earlier chapters, the reason you drink doesn't go away with the booze.

WHAT A HEALTHY RELATIONSHIP LOOKS LIKE

I had no idea what a healthy relationship looked like until I quit drinking. Learning how to advocate for myself opened my eyes to the ways I was mistreated and disrespected in the past. I now have a high bar for all relationships—including friends and family! I'm also getting better at communicating, and adhering to, my own boundaries. Here are a few questions to keep in mind as you start the same journey:

- ❤ Can you be honest with your partner?

- ❤ Do they support your desire to drink less, or fully abstain from alcohol?

- ❤ Can you have difficult conversations without them belittling you, shaming you, or being mean to you?

- 💜 Do you provide that same safe space for them?

- 💜 Do you have mutual trust in each other?

- 💜 Do each of you feel like equals in both the relationship and shared household duties?

- 💜 Do you respect each other?

- 💜 If your answer to any of these questions is no and you want it to be yes, do you feel comfortable discussing that with them?

The following are signs of an *unhealthy* or abusive relationship:

- 💜 Do you invade each other's privacy (going through each other's phone, email, or personal items)?

- 💜 Do they encourage you to drink when you've made it clear that you don't want to?

- 💜 Do they try to keep you away from your friends and family?

- 💜 Do they show up, uninvited, to your work or social settings to cause a scene?

- 💜 Do they tell you that you're crazy for bringing up that things need to change?

- 💜 Do you hurt each other physically, verbally, or emotionally? (If you're being hurt *or* hurting someone else in any way, please look up your local domestic violence hotline for help. People who are concerned about their own behavior toward a partner can still call the hotline.)

If you're changing your relationship with alcohol while already in a relationship with another person, you may find that your perspective shifts, and aspects of your relationship that previously seemed fine are now troubling to you. Cutting back on drinking may also bring out some unhealthy behaviors in your partner, like getting defensive about their own drinking or undermining you. You should keep your deal breakers in mind, but unhealthy behaviors during a time of upheaval don't necessarily spell doom. As long as you're not being hurt or hurting someone else, you can keep reevaluating your relationship over time as you settle into a new interaction with booze. The most important feature of a healthy relationship is communication: if something is happening that you don't like, can you talk it out and commit to change?

Moments of Connection

It's natural to want to get on the same page with someone before you get emotionally or physically intimate. Grabbing a drink is an easy shortcut here, just like on first dates. In an intimacy context, sharing a drink is about more than just booze. It's also a shared experience that might help people connect mentally before connecting physically. But that shared activity doesn't need to involve alcohol. It's actually better if alcohol's not involved so each person can be fully present enough to express enthusiastic consent.

The point here is to establish intentional time that helps each of you transition from the stress of everyday life to being with someone that excites you. Instead of uncorking a cabernet after a long day, try connecting with your mate(s) using one of these exercises:

- **Sync your breath.** Inhaling and exhaling simultaneously can help each of you feel connected to one another. Shared breath work can be a mindful alternative to shared sangria. Even taking one deep breath together can be a nice reset. Take this exercise one step deeper by adding eye contact!

- **Split a pot of tea.** This date night idea can also be used as an intimacy connection exercise. Make a pot of herbal tea. (Maybe implement some of the herbal aphrodisiacs from Chapter 7!) Maybe y'all buy a special teapot for connection time. Not a tea person? Implement the nonalcoholic drink of your choice—even if it's just a seltzer.

- **Do an activity together.** We bond with others through shared experiences. Try cooking together, working out together, or doing a ten-minute meditation.

KEEP THE PASSION ALIVE

I used to conflate *passion* with *drama* when I was drinking. I thought the more dramatic the relationship, the more passionate, and the more the person loved me. That couldn't be further from the truth. My podcast cohost, Lisa Smith, agrees: "Conscious coupling doesn't have to mean forever coupling. But it might. When alcohol is a big feature in a relationship, it's easy to get caught up in, 'Was I too drunk last night? What is the other person thinking? Do they love me? Are they going to leave me?' In a healthy relationship, these fear-based questions don't arise in the same way. Every date is not an all-or-nothing, you-love-me-or-we're-breaking-up drama. You can both make present, conscious decisions as the bigger picture questions arise." I traded in those soap opera fights for calm, adult conversation—and creative outlets that let me lean into my dramatic side, so I don't need to bring it into my relationship.

Chapter 3 suggested some alcohol-free date ideas for igniting passion early in a relationship. But what about some daily or weekly activities to keep that spark alive without imbibing? Each of you will continue to grow individually and as a team. Make sure that you're growing together by staying in touch through communication and including each other in new hobbies as they pop up.

Sometimes passion looks like supporting your beloved in what they're obsessed with. Nick is a member of Soh Daiko, a New York City taiko drumming ensemble. This group is a way for him to stay inspired creatively and stay passionate about drumming. Watching him perform for the first time brought tears to my eyes. I got to watch him thrive in his element, plus he felt supported knowing I was there cheering him on.

Nick knows that I'm obsessed with the thriving nonalcoholic drink scene, so he attends nonalcoholic drink events with me. He makes sure that the restaurants we eat at have nonalcoholic drinks—not just sodas and virgin piña coladas. He's also a kick-ass "Instagram boyfriend" who knows that I need him to take several photos of all these yummy drinks!

In Chapter 1, we talked about how dating yourself is a great way to stay connected with your passions. The more I nurture my own passions, the happier and more confident I feel. Those positive feelings help me feel invigorated in my romantic relationship, too. Irina Gonzalez is a sober journalist, wife, and mama who also advocates for the importance of dating yourself when you're in a relationship. "Fulfilling ourselves on an individual level makes my husband and I more excited to connect as a couple," she shared with me. "Dating ourselves also gives us more to talk about!"

Passion is so much more than rip-off-your-clothes-and-do-me-on-the-kitchen-table sex like we see in movies. Here are a few ways to redefine what passion means to you, individually, and y'all as a team:

- 💜 Talk about what the word *passion* means to each of you. Where do you align? Do you disagree? Does discussing your different definitions help you see passion in a new light?

- 💜 What activities make you feel passionate about your loved one(s)?

- 💜 Did/does alcohol intersect with your passion? How so? Do you feel more passionate while drinking?

- 💜 Do you feel more passionate without alcohol?

SEX ISN'T EVERYTHING

While it's important to keep passion in your relationship, the physical expression of passion—that is, sex—may not be as important as we're told. Sure, sex can be a fun way to self-express, receive and give pleasure, or connect with people you care about. But sex is a small part of what makes a relationship work—if the relationship even includes sex at all. We established earlier that some relationships have no sex and are perfectly valid and healthy.

"People use sex as a relationship barometer because it is definitive," Amanda White, the social-media-savvy therapist from Chapter 1, told me. "You can count the number of times you had sex, [whereas] it's harder to come up with a barometer of how you feel with your partner." Tangibility is a practical measuring tool because we, as humans, like to see results (why do you think power-washing YouTube channels are so popular?), but sex isn't the only way we can gauge intimacy. Here are a few other barometers for a healthy relationship:

- ❤ Date nights: Counting your date nights (look back at Chapter 3 for some creative, booze-free date ideas!) is way more fun than counting the number of times you've had sex this week.

- ❤ Meaningful conversations: Are your conversations with your partner or partners becoming more meaningful since you're drinking less? Take time to reflect on that. Share this discovery with your partner(s), too!

- ❤ Trying new things: Make a commitment to exploring something new together and then track your progress. For instance, you might keep track of the nonalcoholic drinks you test out, with tasting notes on each. Maybe you're nerdy like me and love spreadsheets. Or perhaps you create a ritual to accompany each new drink you try, like having specific glassware designated for your new nonalcoholic beer hobby.

That said, if you and your partner are both allosexual, there's nothing wrong with looking at frequency or regularity of sex as a measure of relationship health! Pay attention to changes, rather than benchmarks—it doesn't matter how often other people have sex or how often is supposedly normal, it matters when something abruptly changes or when there's a mismatch between you. And remember that the following activities can be just as important as penetration:

- ❤ Oral sex

- ❤ Mutual masturbation

- ❤ Fingering

- ❤ Letting your partner(s) help you or watch you masturbate

- ❤ Dry humping (the real thing, no pun)

- ❤ Experimenting with sex toys

- ❤ Phone sex or cybersex

- ❤ Teasing or edging

- ❤ Sensual massage

It's also common for more established relationships to have less sex than newer ones. In new relationships, mutual physical attraction may be one of the few things you have in common. As time goes by and you build a life together, you develop shared interests that compete with sex for time—but also give you other ways to feel close and connected. You'll also learn how to tackle the not-so-sexy stuff like paying bills, experiencing grief, and weathering illness. During challenging periods, sex may be the furthest thing from your mind, but that doesn't mean your relationship isn't strong.

The older I get, the less value I assign to sex. Or maybe I just think about sex differently. I now value intimacy, communication, and snuggling as much as, if not more than, sexual acts. Maybe it's sobriety. Maybe I'm just tired.

CHAPTER 11

DEVELOPING CLEAR COMMUNICATION AND BOOZE-FREE ARGUING

When you merge your lives together, a lot of uncomfortable emotions may arise. Your partner has a whole life and career outside of your relationship, and you do too; love doesn't mean that these independent lives mesh seamlessly. For me, moving in with Nick brought up some repressed issues I didn't know existed. For instance, in the past I had rarely nested because it felt pointless. My mom and I moved frequently growing up, so I subconsciously repeated the same habits, moving every one to two years in adulthood. I usually lived with roommates or partners who already had furniture or moved into furnished apartments, and to this day, I only own one piece of furniture. Plus, the one time I'd tried nesting, the relationship ended badly. All this meant that I panicked when Nick and I rolled out our new bedroom rug. I ran to the kitchen, hyperventilating and freaking out. Nick held me as I cried, listening to how I felt. Then I processed these new emotions with my therapist. I'm so grateful I didn't drink to get through that discomfort. Instead, I shared my feelings with my partner and a mental health professional.

If you were already in a relationship before considering getting sober or drinking less, you've likely already weathered some uncomfortable conversations with your current partner or partners. They may have already seen you at your worst: drunk fights, saying mean things you regret in the morning, or holding your hair back while promising the porcelain gods that you'll never drink again. But changing how alcohol shows up in your relationship means learning how to fight sober, make up sober, and have the real courage to make real changes together. That may feel very different.

When I still drank, I had no idea how to argue correctly. I thought fighting was bad, so I often kicked issues under the rug, pretending that the bumps were part of the room's décor (a pseudo attempt at nesting, if you will). I lacked the self-awareness to articulate my feelings, but I sure knew how to drunkenly show up slurring and sobbing at a boyfriend's doorstep because he wasn't returning my calls. You don't need to quit drinking to have productive communication with your partner or partners. But alcohol does make it harder to think clearly, actively listen, evaluate your emotions, and express your needs.

Alcohol can create communication barriers whether someone is a social drinker or a self-identified alcoholic. "Clear communication is essential for a healthy relationship," says Keegan Herring, the queer mindfulness-based therapist from Chapter 9. "Even the occasional drinker can still black out, initiating fights that they don't remember which often leaves a lasting impact on their partner." Communication is akin to being vulnerable in a relationship, and many people use alcohol to avoid vulnerability, inhibiting communication. We sometimes spin such an elaborate web just to have a damn drink.

Getting alcohol out of your conflicts may also help you decide when to stop fighting and walk away. When I was drinking I saw romantic partners as projects. Sobriety, therapy, and learning about codependency taught me that these "fixer-upper" opportunities were really red flags. I had so little self-esteem that I thought I needed liquid courage to feel confident, yet I also put myself on such a pedestal that I thought it was my job to fix other people. Perhaps having a relationship project was a coping skill, a way to deflect my issues.

I've since learned that we must meet people where they are. They'll grow or evolve at their own pace, just like you. And it's not your responsibility to monitor the speed at which they go through life. But it is your responsibility to ensure you're OK with riding this ride, even if it never evolves—and to get off the ride if you aren't.

Giving up booze gave me the headspace to learn some effective communication tools. That same clear headspace also helped me see dates and partners for who they are instead of who I wanted them to be, removing a huge impetus for fights in past relationships.

YOU CAN STILL HAVE A GIRLS' NIGHT

There is still a great deal of uncertainty even after you've met *the one* (or the *however many*). Questions might arise such as: *When are we getting married? Do I even want to get married? Will they ever learn to clean up after themselves? Is this seriously how they want to decorate our home?* These are excellent topics to explore with your close friends (and of course, your therapist!).

Moving away from alcohol doesn't mean you can't have a girls' night (or whatever gender your friends are) to commiserate about the challenges that sometimes arise when people are in love. Just try it with seltzer, juice, or nonalcoholic rosé. This way you stay fully present to listen to what your friends are going through *and* you can remember the advice they give you. Getting drunk and complaining is just a vent session if you aren't able to hear and implement advice. Venting with people you love and trust can be fulfilling in its own right, but why not try something mindful and constructive?

- ❤ If you usually gather with your friends over wine, grab a few bottles of the nonalcoholic stuff. You'll be surprised to discover that much of the satisfaction of sharing a bottle of wine is in the ritual rather than the drink's alcohol content. Popping a cork, then pouring your drink into wineglasses still provides that comforting sense of calmness. If fake alcohol isn't your thing, stock up on seltzer or make a yummy wine-free sangria with fresh fruit and juices.

- ❤ Set the vibe with calming accoutrements. If you want a chill, witchy atmosphere, grab some incense, crystals, and tarot cards. For a modern moment, try soothing face masks, a kick-ass playlist, and fresh flowers. It's *your* vent session, so you can set the tone that fits your current mood.

❤ Explore the following prompts with your friends. Maybe you each write in a journal and share the writing. Maybe you just go around in a circle, talking about how the prompts make you feel.

➤ My partner(s) and I are fighting about . . .

➤ I see the situation this way . . .

➤ My partner sees it this way . . .

➤ We disagree on . . .

➤ The emotions I feel about this disagreement are . . .

Mindfully discussing these prompts can help you process emotions and empathize. Processing with people you trust can help you decide what to say (and not say!) to your partner or partners when you fight.

HOW TO FIGHT

Fighting doesn't mean your relationship is in trouble. In fact, a respectful, productive fight can help move a relationship forward—especially when each party has a clear mind and the ability to identify their needs and adequately articulate them. There's no perfectly frictionless relationship, especially if you're sharing space and responsibilities; everyone will have some frustrations or tension. If you're not letting those out, that means someone is withholding or repressing their feelings, and those emotions will eventually blow up. Withheld feelings may foment into resentment or grudges, popping up at an inopportune time.

I discussed this topic with Mary Beth O'Connor, author of *From Junkie to Judge: One Woman's Triumph Over Trauma and Addiction.* She told me the most noticeable change in her relationship over twenty-nine years of sobriety is the "radical reduction in conflict between us and the increase in positive feelings for each other." My experience was similar. Once I learned how to communicate regularly, there were fewer fights, because I was able to broach difficult subjects instead of harboring resentment or holding grudges.

It's natural to want to keep the peace or not ruin a lovely afternoon by bringing up an unpleasant topic, but talking about something important doesn't have to be a large-scale production. I'm often surprised when I psych myself up for a big talk with my partner only to realize that the discussion needed just a few sentences of crystal clear communication and listening to each other. Life continues to happen on life's terms. Here are a few ways to communicate with your partner or partners instead of hoping that a glass of wine will magically erase your current complaint.

THE SITUATION: You're upset about something they did or said and feel the need to discuss it ASAP.

AVOID: Approaching them randomly. "I can't believe that you ____! What were you thinking?"

TRY THIS: "Can we chat about _____ when you get a chance?"

The "when you get a chance" is crucial here. Adding those five little words to your request can work wonders. You've made it clear that you want to talk about something, then put the ball in their court to come to you. Nick tells me that adding "when you get a chance" gives him time to prepare for our conversation while finishing what he's working on. "Sometimes I want to finish what I'm doing, even if I'm just watching a video, before diving into something else," he said. "Adding 'when you get a chance' lets me put our conversation on my list; then we can talk when we're both ready, rather than dropping what I'm doing to talk immediately."

Better yet, ask your partner (during a chill time) the best way to approach them. A few months ago, Nick told me he preferred that I email him about household chores. We agreed on a reasonable time for him to complete the task in question. You may be surprised to learn that your communication style evolves like your taste in food.

THE SITUATION: They're not doing something you want them to do in the time frame you want them to.

AVOID: "Why haven't you washed the dishes yet? The sink is full, and my favorite coffee mug is on the bottom." The accusatory tone suggests that there's no right answer to "why haven't you"—your coffee cup is more important than their reason for not washing it.

TRY THIS: "Do you think you can commit to washing the dishes at night? Walking into a clean kitchen in the morning helps me start my day right."

This works because it focuses on the positive outcome when they do the task at the time you'd prefer, and emphasizes why that's important to you. Be prepared to hear reasons why that won't work for *them*, and perhaps even to swap chore responsibilities if your timing needs don't match up.

THE SITUATION: You're frustrated by a habit of theirs.

AVOID: "You always leave your socks on the floor!" Nobody wants to feel micromanaged, especially by their beloved, *especially* in their own home. Speaking in absolutes like "you always" or "you never" is likely to make them defensive, since it's rarely completely true. Then you wind up fighting over whether they really *always* do it, instead of about the substance of your complaint.

TRY THIS: "When you _____, I feel _____."

Again, focus on why the behavior matters to you, rather than starting from the assumption that they're doing something obviously wrong. This allows you to communicate your feelings to your partner without sounding accusatory. They have no reason not to leave their socks on the floor if you haven't communicated why you care! In early sobriety or sober curiosity, you'll be discovering a lot of your feelings. This is a great chance to share them with your beloved.

When I was depressed and drank heavily, I didn't care what my home looked like. But in sobriety, I've found that a messy home affects my mental health. I've had to explicitly let my partner know what I need our home to look like, and acknowledge that it's changed. We had a talk, agreed on what we both want from our domestic space, and doled out the chores to make it possible. This is why it's essential to establish a baseline.

If you are accustomed to loud and angry fighting, some of these calmer alternatives may feel artificial and unsatisfying at first! But while yelling may be familiar (and maybe even cathartic), you'll find that it's easier to actually address and fix a problem that you've discussed more calmly. Keeping the energy at a simmer instead of a boil allows everyone to feel heard while also leaving you in full control of your emotions.

Pick Your Battles

We've all heard "pick your battles" as standard relationship advice, but how do we pick our battles? "Many couples think it's me versus them, when it's really us versus the problem," therapist Amanda White reminded me. Once you identify the problem for what it is, instead of making it a referendum on your whole relationship, it can be easier to pick your battles. Remember that you and your partner(s) are a team! If the problem is dishes in the sink, it's not me versus Nick, it's us versus the dishes. How can we, as a team, create a system so the dishes are washed regularly?

Here are some things to consider when picking your own battles:

- Is it easier to just do the thing (take out the trash, clean the toilet, make the kid's lunch) than it is to ask them why they haven't done it?

- How urgent is this issue? Can the discussion happen later in the day or tomorrow once you've had some distance?

- Are you making this issue mean something that it doesn't? I'm guilty of this! My therapist helped me understand that Nick forgetting to wash the dishes doesn't mean anything more than he forgot to wash the dishes. My resentments made a sink of dishes manifest into my own "Nick doesn't respect me" story. Once I communicated the importance of having a clean sink in our home, he understood where I came from, and we created a system to make sure those dishes are washed.

- Can you agree to disagree? This is a standard cliché for a reason. You're different people who won't see eye to eye on everything. Is debating worth your time and energy?

- Consider a few communication options. If you're fired up and a talk might escalate into a shouting match, try writing down how you feel or going for a walk to clear your head. Maybe you text each other about the fight from different rooms. The physical distance can create a safe barrier while typing can give you a chance to write out, and edit, your thoughts before hitting send.

- Remember that you're not in this alone! Call a friend or trusted family member to hear an objective perspective—or just to vent. Talking it out with someone else before you rehash the issue with your beloved might help you figure out what you really want to say and avoid saying something you regret.

- Hit pause on the fight to talk about something else. Taking a breather to do something you both love can bring some much-needed levity to a heavy situation. It can also remind you why you love each other, making that fight feel unnecessary after all.

- Consider a compromise. In dialectical behavioral therapy, it's common to discuss how two opposing ideas can be true at once. Maybe you and your partner(s) are each correct and y'all can make this duality work by reaching a compromise.

- Maybe they're right. I know, I know. This one's tough. But consider it as a thought experiment.

BE PROACTIVE

On my first official date with Nick, I mentioned how important it is that my person is open to proactive couples' therapy. I think a lot of people might have been freaked out by that request, especially so early in the relationship. But Nick and I met in AA and we'd already passed typical first date conversation hours before.

Now, Nick and I have quarterly sessions with a couples' therapist. We don't keep a list of topics to discuss in couples' therapy. We communicate regularly, so therapy rarely has surprises. Our sessions are just a safe space to talk and hear a professional perspective.

I realize preventative couples' therapy may be a foreign concept to many—hell, it was for me not too long ago. But I share this because giving up alcohol or drinking less offers us a time to get present, which in turn helps us show up in our relationships in new ways.

If couples' therapy is a "hell no" for you, here are a few other ways to be proactive in your relationship in sobriety or sober curiosity:

- ❤ Designate one hour each week to talk about the tedious stuff. Having a time slot dedicated for communication can help each of you compartmentalize your thoughts throughout the week. It can also let you rest assured that you won't be randomly bombarded with "Hey, can we talk?" while reading on the couch. The longer you practice communicating, the less you'll need that designated hour! (Disclaimer: Some issues are absolutely worth interrupting for and may even require frequent discussion. You and your partner(s) can gauge how to go about this approach.)

- ❤ Communicate your boundaries around alcohol with your partner. Let them know if you don't want to be around them when they're drinking or you want to take a break from attending parties with alcohol.

❤ If one or both of you drink, commit to *not* fighting while either of you is buzzed or intoxicated. Or at the very least, commit to discussing the fight the next day once the alcohol is out of everyone's system. Gigi Engle, the sex educator from Chapter 7, says that taking a few years away from booze helped her learn how to communicate with her husband: "One night recently, my husband and I had some drinks with a couple of our friends. He and I ended up having a serious conversation. And then in the morning I suggested discussing what we talked about the night before. And we had a whole other conversation while sober to get clear on the message. Alcohol just muddles the message. It makes us feel bold to talk about stuff we're scared to talk about. 'Cause you don't feel like there will be repercussions, but it muddles what you're actually trying to say. And so it actually can hinder more than it can help."

❤ Improve your listening skills. Are you fully tuned-in to your partner, or are you usually just waiting for them to stop talking so you can speak your mind?

❤ Ask if they want advice or just want a space to vent. Do you give advice before asking if that's what they want? Is this advice you give tailored to how you would handle the situation versus how you think they should handle it? On the other side of this, when you want to vent, ask your partner if they're available to listen. Maybe they had a stressful day, too, and just want to be alone. Or maybe y'all can make a date of it: "Want to meet on the patio in thirty minutes for a mutual bitch fest? I'll make a pot of tea!" This gives each of you some time to decompress from your day before coming together to talk about why it sucked.

❤ Practice active listening. Repeat back what you just heard. This helps you process what they said and helps them know if what they said was received correctly. Years of working in customer service taught me the value in active listening. People ordered their food or drink, and I repeated it back to them to make sure that, first, I jotted down the right order and, second, they communicated their order correctly. This works in relationships too. It works even better when the people communicating are of sound mind, not inebriated.

Remain open to learning more about your partner or partners and letting them learn more about you. The more you learn about each other, the better you can show up for each other. And the longer you're sober or practicing mindful drinking, the more you'll learn about about how to be present for who you are while in a relationship. "The biggest mistake is believing there is one right way to listen, to talk, to have a conversation—or a relationship," communication expert Dr. Deborah Tannen wrote in *You Just Don't Understand: Women and Men in Conversation*. She wrote that in 1990, but nobody's discovered a single right way of communicating in the thirty-plus years since. In the same way that I recommend not comparing your relationship with alcohol to someone else's, don't compare your romantic relationships to someone else's. Communicate in the way that makes the most sense for *you*.

Communication is like flexing a muscle: the more you do it, the stronger you both become. What was once a feat of strength becomes a simple dialogue. Of course Nick and I still fight, but we now have more constructive conversations and fewer shouting matches. Withholding your feelings may also be a sign of people pleasing, which manifests elsewhere in relationships. The best way to please people is to be your genuine self. Following your intrinsic courage gets you there.

CHAPTER 12

SURVIVING A BREAKUP WITHOUT THE BOOZE

Breakups are one of the most devastating losses we can go through. Ending a significant relationship can feel overwhelming, even when you're the one who calls things off. If relationships are filled with love, meaningful moments, and inside jokes, then what fills a breakup? For a lot of people, it's booze. Taking time to evaluate how alcohol intersects with dating, sex, and romance also includes mindfully mourning the end of a relationship.

I spoke with quit lit icon Holly Whitaker, the author of *Quit Like a Woman: the Radical Choice to Not Drink in a Culture Obsessed With Alcohol*, about the benefits of processing a breakup without alcohol. "Nothing is more destroying for me, and harder to manage or navigate, than a breakup," she told me. "If I were to drink through it, I would make it such a big mess—but then there's the other part of it, which is that the value of being alive is that we can feel so much. I know even though I don't want [the pain] to be happening, that it is really, really precious ground and that I can face it. I choose to be there for myself when I'm most in need, to feel the fullness of the experience that a human being can have. It's lucky." Just like liquid courage provides fleeting confidence, drinking through the pain is temporary, too. In fact, you often just end up with a killer hangover to go with your broken heart.

As with dating, it takes a lot of intrinsic courage to resist the cultural pressure to opt for these temporary fixes. Not only are you encouraged to meet dates and sexual partners in bars, but you're also expected to grieve those relationships in the very same environment. We've all seen the movies where the protagonist goes through a breakup and their BFF drags them to a bar to get wasted and flirt with someone new—maybe even to hook up with a random person. This is usually the cheesy part of the storyline where the BFF character says something like, "The best way to get over someone is to get under someone else," then winks while handing the protagonist a shot, gesturing to the hot person who happens to be looking their way.

The 2019 Netflix film *Someone Great* follows music journalist Jenny, portrayed by Gina Rodriguez, around New York City for a day as she processes a breakup. We see Jenny and her friends day-drink while wandering the city. Jenny drinks whiskey from the bottle with two straws, dancing to Lizzo one minute, then crying the next. We later see her mixing champagne with green juice, a sort of breakup mimosa. In the 2008 movie *Forgetting Sarah Marshall* we see Jason Segal's character, Peter, mourn his breakup with the eponymous Sarah Marshall by comedically binging "girly drinks" such as cosmopolitans and piña coladas, then crying himself to sleep—only to wake up and order rum with his breakfast.

I wondered if alcohol is needed to make those scenes relatable or funny, so I chatted with documentary filmmaker and Notre Dame professor Ted Mandell. He codeveloped a course called "Drunk on Film" where he and social psychologist Anré Venter examine the psychology and seduction of alcohol on screen. "Drunkenness as comedy is a go-to narrative device," Mandell told me. "Absolutely those film scenes could be alcohol-free . . . but the physical comedy would be lost. And the comedy is what's numbing the pain in these two films. If you want your audience to laugh, just write a scene where your protagonist gets drunk. So it's really about how the director wants the audience to feel." Still, there's no reason the director couldn't use a breakup scene differently, Mandell suggested. "Wouldn't it be cool if staying sober in these situations was a narrative moment? A scene where the protagonist is confronted with alcohol, the friend takes them out to forget about getting dumped, then they reject the alcohol?" Now that's a nuanced scene I'd love to see on-screen! Perhaps I, too, used drunkenness as a narrative device to help me get through the hard times, before I learned how to take life one day at a time.

NUMBING VERSUS DISTRACTION

When we hurt, physically or emotionally, our lizard brains tell us to shut the pain down by any means possible. But as an evolved species, we're *supposed* to sometimes feel emotional pain—that's how we grow. If you're experiencing normal, necessary, ultimately beneficial pain, like from a breakup, it's better to distract yourself than to try to numb the pain away—especially if your go-to numbing solution is alcohol.

"Distraction is intentional. There is a specific reason for distraction," says Amanda White, the therapist from Chapter 1. "We wouldn't be able to lead a productive life if we felt our feelings 24/7." White recommends setting a time to occupy yourself instead of drinking while also distracting yourself from grief. "If you feel like you want to drink, watch a show for an hour or go for an hour-long walk," she suggests. "Distract yourself for a certain period of time. It can be a really healthy way to increase your pain tolerance." Intentional distraction can be a mindful, beneficial approach to grieving a lost love, since it moves us forward. By contrast, mindlessly numbing can be counterproductive, keeping you stuck in the pain.

It's natural to want to quell the pain or discomfort as you mourn a great love. You take ibuprofen for a headache and antacids for a heartburn, so what do you take for a heartache? To grieve a devastating loss without turning to booze, resist numbing behavior and instead opt for distraction.

INSTEAD OF: Doomscrolling for hours

TRY: Reading a funny or lighthearted book

INSTEAD OF: Drinking mindlessly

TRY: Learning a new dessert recipe

INSTEAD OF: Hiding in bed

TRY: Preparing a relaxing bath with music, candles, etc.

INSTEAD OF: Bingeing trash TV

TRY: Bingeing trash TV, but doing it with a friend

How to Grieve a Lost Love Without Turning to Booze

You don't have to get drunk to alleviate heartbreak. Try one of these booze-free options instead.

- Stay busy with activities, whether it's joining a book club or a running/walking group. Keep your mind and body moving when you need a healthy distraction from the heartache.

- Feel your feelings instead of drowning them in booze. Have a buddy or journal or therapist with whom you feel comfortable discussing those feelings.

- Volunteer at an organization that aligns with your values. Giving back can help you put your current heartache into perspective.

- Invite a friend over for coffee and commiseration. You're not in this alone!

- Revisit the "Dating Yourself" chapter of this book. This is a great time to reconnect with your intrinsic courage before putting yourself out there again.

- Give yourself as much time and grace as you need to process this difficult situation.

- Masturbate. Duh!

TURN YOUR HEARTACHE INTO ART

Giving up alcohol felt like a breakup. I ended a thirteen-year-long affair with Jack Daniels, a bottle of booze that treated me horribly but kept me coming back for more. Some recovery programs ask people to write a breakup letter to their drug of choice as a way to say farewell to the substance that repeatedly broke their heart. My breakup letter took the form of a photo shoot, because I'm an annoying millennial who loves to convert everything into social media likes.

When I was nine months sober, I invited Courtney, a photographer friend, over to document me finally getting rid of my remaining bottle. (Don't ask why I kept it for that long because I truly don't know. Maybe knowing that whiskey was available and choosing not to drink it made me feel strong?) Our photo shoot took place in an alleyway of Jersey City at sunset. Courtney photographed me pouring the booze, along with its empty promises, down the sewage drains. I even smashed the bottle at the end (and cleaned it up!), feeling free now that I was finally over the asshole who treated me like shit. I reflected on how a silly liquid had such a hold over me. How one day I chugged from the bottle, desperate for its contents to activate my confidence, and another day, nine months later, I could throw it all away, finally seeing how useless it was.

There's no reason a romantic breakup can't also be an opportunity for a photo shoot (get those likes!). Or you could process your feelings by writing a song, painting a picture, creating a post-breakup mood board, or even having a ceremonial bonfire. Any of these mindful pursuits, even the silliest, will be more helpful and less destructive than getting drunk.

Katie Mack, the Webby-winning sober podcaster from Chapter 8, is also an actor who turned her breakup story into an interactive one-woman show titled #breakupcontent. "The first step is to acknowledge how fucking awful the pain is and how there's like a small part of you that knows that you're gonna get through it and also thinks that you're not," she told me. "It's the same thing with choosing to drink or not drink. Choosing to drink, you're making a conscious choice to delay any progress. The biggest rebellious act you can do is giving yourself the opportunity to start the healing process."

You don't have to go so far as to write a one-woman show or have a photoshoot with your ex, but here are some other ways to get creative with your heartache:

- ❤ Create a sensual sanctuary. Fill your bathroom with luxurious soaps and floral bouquets, and take a decadent bath or shower. Outfit your bedroom with new pillows, soft blankets, and scented candles (use caution with open flames). You can even bring a cup of tea or a snack into the bath or into bed with you. (You know what's a wonderful, productive creative project? Getting really good at cheese plates.)

- ❤ Create a mood board of your new life. What does post-breakup you look like? How do you dress? If you live together with the person you've broken up with, what will your new apartment look like? You can do this on Pinterest or by physically collaging or drawing pictures.

- ❤ Purge. Have a small, contained fire where you burn a memento (make sure it's safely flammable!) or a symbolic note or drawing. Or clean them out of your life: pour anger (and detergent) onto any surfaces that remind you of your ex. Do what you can to remove their scent, random pubes, various belongings, and negative energy. This might also be a good time to donate any clothing that reminds you of your ex.

❤ Seek stability. Finding your footing after an earth-shattering loss can make anyone feel dizzy, so it's best to try to keep up as much routine as possible. Even if it's just brushing your teeth at the same time every day.

IDENTIFY THE PAIN

Sobriety helped me realize that numbing my emotional pain is a learned behavior. Those thirteen years of consistent substance abuse contained quite a few breakups. Whether they were official relationships or casual situationships, they still hurt once they ended. But I never let myself feel that pain. "Breakups hurt—with or without substances. This is when numbing out or avoiding your feelings feels tantalizing," Paulina Pinsky, the sober writer you met in Chapter 1, shared with me. "But in reality, the more you avoid the feeling, the more fiercely it will bubble up later. If you don't sit down to breathe and swallow the emotion, it will come and fight you later down the line. Ride the wave, even if it hurts." Drunk me never sat with an emotion long enough to analyze it. Sober me can assess how I feel by asking the following questions:

❤ What is this feeling? Properly identifying the crappy feelings that come with a breakup helps you process them better than pretending you don't feel them at all.

❤ What else do I feel? I like to name my crappy feelings because it reminds me that even though this particular emotional state feels all-consuming, it's actually just a part of how I feel. That recognition brings me back to reality, helping me feel balanced. Sure, I feel devastated, but I also feel hungry or nauseated or grouchy or annoyed. Nurturing those other feelings can pull me out of bed, even if it's just to get a snack.

- 💜 Why does it suck? Sometimes a feeling sucks because it reminds me of a dark time in my past. Sometimes it sucks because it's a brand-new feeling, or maybe it's a feeling I haven't felt without alcohol yet.

- 💜 What's behind this feeling? There's a saying in recovery: "Nobody is ever mad, they just don't let themselves feel sad." That resonates deeply with me as someone who's more in touch with anger and rage than sadness and tears.

When I'm too exhausted to do that emotional work, I hit pause on my brain and press play on whichever show I'm streaming. I'll resume the emotional effort when I'm ready, or bring it up with my therapist. If sobriety teaches me anything, it's that life is worth living. I want to be present for what happens. Now that alcohol is out of my life, I feel (and process) life as it comes. From the devastating heartaches to the heart-bursting romantic moments to the career highs and lows. I'm here for it all.

CHAPTER 13

BUILDING A MINDFULLY COURAGEOUS LOVE LIFE

Dating, sex, and relationships are complex; each stage requires deep levels of vulnerability. There's the scariness of putting yourself out there on the first few dates, but then there are those tummy-tingling moments when the date goes really well. This is followed by the grab bag of emotions that arise as those tummy tingles morph into L-O-V-E. And possibly the truest form of exposure comes from sharing what intimacy means to each of you individually, and then discovering what intimacy means to you as a team. Plus, of course, there's the possibility that it all goes to shit somewhere along the way.

At any point on that emotional roller coaster, it's perfectly natural to reach for something like alcohol to find the courage to face your fears. But what if drinkers could tap into their intrinsic courage so easily that they never needed to outsource that confidence to alcohol in the first place? What if they only reached for a drink if they truly wanted it, not because they thought they needed it to feel sexy or confident? More and more people are looking for ways to make this dream a reality. Perhaps booze-free life will be so prevalent that our great-grandkids will wonder why we looked for courage in a bottle, in the same way that we don't understand how our great-grandparents made it to events on time without iCal notifications.

REINVEST IN YOURSELF
AND YOUR RELATIONSHIPS

I couldn't build a courageous life without acknowledging my sordid past with alcohol and how those choices impact where I am today. I made peace with those choices by taking an honest look—and doing some math. I made some brutal calculations that estimate how much time, money, and energy I gave to alcohol, keeping me closer to liquid courage and distanced from intrinsic courage. You can do your own calculations or learn from mine!

Financial Costs

By now, you're aware of alcohol's physical and emotional side effects, but have you ever thought about the financial side effects? Calculating how much money I spent on alcohol is one of the most sobering exercises I did in early recovery. On average, I went out for drinks three nights a week for ten years, spending about $50 a night.

$50 × 3 nights = $150 per week

$150 × 4 weeks = $600 per month

$600 × 12 months = $7,200 per year

$7,200 × 10 years = $72,000

Yes, you read that right. I spent *at least* $72,000 on getting hammered. This figure does not reflect the late-night tacos or the countless morning-after pills, or the after-hours party favors that seemed like a good idea when I was wasted

Energy Costs

The first time I heard someone use the term *energy budget* it blew my mind. I knew how to budget my money (even thought I didn't— sorry, Grandpa!), but I never thought to budget my time and energy until I got sober. My average nights out were four-hour increments.

$$4 \text{ hours} \times 3 \text{ nights} = 12 \text{ hours a week}$$
$$12 \text{ hours} \times 4 \text{ weeks} = 48 \text{ hours per month}$$
$$48 \text{ hours} \times 12 \text{ months} = 576 \text{ hours per year}$$
$$576 \text{ hours} \times 10 \text{ years} = 5{,}760 \text{ hours}$$

No wonder I struggled in school; I spent the same amount of time in the bar as I did in class. I now spend that time reading books, catching up with friends, working out, having booze-free fun dates with my beloved, and writing this book!

Now it's your turn. Take a deep breath, then do some scary math. Don't beat yourself up! Instead, think about what you can do with those resources now that you're claiming them back. I jokingly refer to that $72,000 as a research grant that led me to become the Sober Sexpert. What could you do, in your personal life and your romantic life, if you had an extra $72,000 and 5,760 hours (or whatever numbers you come up with) to invest in yourself and your dates or relationships? Would you take a date to that hot new restaurant? Go on a weeklong vacation with your main squeeze? Get those shoes that have been following you around the internet? Take a cooking class with someone you're excited about? This exercise is *not* designed to beat yourself up. It's to remind you that quitting or cutting back on alcohol gives you back time and money, not just intangible things like courage and control.

GET QUIET

Early sobriety or sober curiosity often comes with a side of mindfulness. That doesn't have to mean attending a silent meditation retreat in the woods. Mindfulness can also mean looking at yourself, your habits, and your surroundings in a new light. It means treating your body and mind with respect and kindness. Mindfulness can also mean observing life, taking a walk, cooking dinner, listening to music, or snuggling with your little ones (human or animal).

I have a theory that the rising ubiquity of Eastern philosophy, yoga, and meditation in the West is why we are seeing a consistent increase in sober curiosity and dry dating recently. This newfound awareness is everywhere in our lives, especially in romantic relationships. Perhaps this is why people in the West now eat less meat, recycle more, shop more sustainably, and drink less booze. Some yoga practitioners view the human body as a vessel, a temporary container that gets a spirit from point A to point B. What if we looked at liquid courage the same way? Maybe liquid courage brought us to this point in our lives, and we don't need it anymore.

The essence of mindfulness is slowness and gratitude. Before you gag from all the annoying buzzwords I just dropped, listen to what Dr. Anadel Baughn Barbour, a psychiatrist and the author of *Sex in Sobriety: A Qualitative Narrative Exploration of the Utilization of Mindfulness Practices for Enjoyable Sober Sex*, posits in her book. "Using mind-altering substances during childhood and adolescence could effect chemical changes to the brain, creating emotional distortions in the mind resulting in unhealthy sexual experiences lasting into adulthood," she writes. "Combining meditation and yoga creates a connection between the mind and body, providing present-time awareness. Present-time awareness is an important component to enjoyable sober sex." As you know from reading this far, Dr. Barbour might as well be describing my relationship with alcohol, sex, and love.

Perhaps sober sex truly can be better when integrated with mindfulness. If you're thinking, "I'm not about to fucking meditate," I'm right there with you. While I'm more relaxed and patient with regular meditation practice, I still have a love-hate relationship with it. But practicing mindfulness doesn't have to mean accepting all the woo-woo stuff that sometimes comes with it (unless you like the woo-woo stuff), and it doesn't have to mean self-denial. Mindfulness is about present-time awareness. The awareness you woke up to while dating yourself, while having fun booze-free dates, while asking for what you want in bed, and effectively communicating with someone you're into. All of that is possible because you replaced liquid courage with intrinsic courage. Where alcohol pulled me away from myself, mindful, intrinsic courage keeps me closer to my truth instead of trying to live someone else's.

If you're allergic to the word *mindfulness*, try saying present-time awareness, or stillness. Whatever you call it, I actively avoided it when I drank. Now I can see how avoiding myself resulted in unhealthy sexual and romantic relationship patterns. I relied on liquid courage to do all the work for me. My relationship with *relationships* only improved once I got present and sober.

Now I know that I must put in the work to tap into, and maintain, my intrinsic courage, and it's 100 percent worth it.

FIND YOUR PLACEBO

I get a lot of questions from people who are curious about removing alcohol from their sex life, dating, and relationships, and they all have one connective thread: people want an equal replacement for booze, a quick one-to-one substitution. They never like that my answer is always no. And that's the whole point. There's no quick fix—that's why many of us drink in the first place. I got drunk to prepare for the sex I didn't always want, and stayed drunk to get through relationships that weren't right for me—to do any of this without booze would have required figuring out why I was essentially drugging myself into complacency. The only true replacement for booze is rolling up your sleeves to figure out why you reach for the drink in the first place.

Once you've figured that out, though, and even while you're working on getting it nailed down, there's nothing wrong with using a symbolic shortcut. Develop habits for relationship pain points—pre-date jitters, post-fight malaise, whatever—that encourage mindfulness and help you remember to tap into intrinsic courage. A meditative pre-date skin care or face massage routine, for instance, isn't a direct substitute for booze, because it won't forcibly calm your brain and your nerves. But you can use it to remind yourself to slow down and recognize all the internal resources you already have.

Way back at the beginning of this book, I mentioned Raj from the sitcom *The Big Bang Theory*, who is unable to talk to women unless he has a beer first. As the show progresses, we see that his character struggles with social anxiety, which manifests as selective mutism. As he learns to address his anxiety directly, he stops feeling the need to self-medicate with alcohol. There's a scene in a later season where Raj discovers that, while feeling confident talking to a woman, he's actually drinking nonalcoholic beer. The placebo effect worked on him, activating the intrinsic courage he had all along.

My journey has been similar to Raj's, in that I used alcohol as a shortcut to feeling confident in an area I felt deeply insecure about: relationships. Receiving professional help got me a mental health diagnosis, correct medication, and tools for communication. Getting to know the real me inherently unlocked my intrinsic courage.

Dumbo didn't need the feather. Raj didn't need the beer. You and I don't need them either.

THE COURAGE TO CHANGE

At some point in your life you've probably encountered the Serenity Prayer: "God, grant me the serenity to accept the things I cannot change, the courage to change the things I can, and the wisdom to know the difference." I struggle with the words *God* and *prayer*, but I think of the Serenity Prayer as a song lyric that helps me make sense of the world. The prayer was originally written by theologian and ethicist Reinhold Niebuhr in the early 1930s, but it's become a mainstay in Alcoholics Anonymous and other twelve-step programs because of the way it encourages thoughtful change without spinning your wheels. Though I'm not a twelve-stepper, I remind myself of this prayer daily, sometimes several times—minus the "God" part. (There's a translation of the prayer into Klingon, the constructed language from *Star Trek*, that replaces "God grant me" with "may I find." Less spiritual types, and *Star Trek* fans, may prefer that one.)

The key point of the Serenity Prayer is that feeling serene requires both acceptance *and* courage. Niebuhr isn't talking about artificial courage that only works when your prefrontal cortex *doesn't*. He's talking about real, intrinsic courage to change what you can change. So as we work to build a mindful, grounded, complete love life without relying on alcohol, it helps to think about both what we should accept and what we can have the courage to change.

Acceptance

💜 Accept people where they are. If your date insists on meeting in a bar, you can decide they're not for you, rather than needing to convince or change them.

💜 Accept yourself where you are. If you're going to be awkward and weird on a date if you don't have a drink first, great, be awkward and weird! Someone will find it charming, guaranteed. If that person isn't your date, then commit to being charmed by your awkward self.

💜 *Don't* try to fix someone who might have a drinking problem. *Do* decide if that's a person you want to be around.

💜 Remember that people who are deeply in love can still have bad sex sometimes, and people who have bad sex can still be deeply in love. Nick and I still have awkward dates and we still laugh through the awkwardness of trying something new in bed. I now accept that type of humility makes our relationship stronger.

Courage

❤ To live a life filled with intrinsic courage is to remember what you enjoy about this life. Do as much of what brings you joy as possible. Increase your endorphins. Try new things. Ask for help when shit gets hard. And know that you don't need alcohol to get through a tough time or celebrate the good times.

❤ Living an authentically courageous life leaves you susceptible to teasing because you're living life against the grain. Your date may have opinions if you politely decline a drink, but hey, someone who's judging you for not drinking will probably also weigh in if you drink too much. If you're going to take shit for something, should it be for a conscious, mindful choice?

❤ By now you know the difference between channeling your genuine, authentic courage in your love life and outsourcing your confidence to the liquid equivalent of a magic feather. This kind of courage requires true honesty and not becoming attached to a specific outcome.

❤ Someone can come across as fantastic on a dating app or seem like the one after only a few dates. But "come across" and "seem" are impressions, not facts. Early impressions rarely tell the full story. Courage here requires a willingness to remain open to revising those impressions as things develop. And if that happens in a way that means this relationship is not going to be safe and happy for you, courage means letting go and moving on.

HANDLING YOUR EMOTIONS

Part of the reason that people in recovery are so interested in *serenity* is that changing your relationship with alcohol can dredge up a whole bunch of feelings. You may recognize past mistreatment for the first time, or you may find that behaviors you used to tolerate now feel like insults. You may find yourself being angry at people who didn't help you before, or people who aren't helping themselves now. And you may find that even normal emotions feel like they're turned up to eleven without the numbing effects of booze.

I spoke with Lucy Hart, an award-winning adult performer and trans activist, about this challenge of living an authentically courageous life without alcohol. "Part of staying sober long-term is being able to deal with resentment and judgment," she told me. "If you can't find a healthy way to process your own resentments and judgments, you're not going to make it. You're going to eventually go back to what 'worked'—which was alcohol and drugs. You have to deal with the acid of resentment that's coursing through your veins." Lucy's words ring true whether you're in long-term recovery or you're sober curious.

There's no top of the proverbial "I'm amazing at dating and relationships!" mountain. Still, there is a glorious, hilly terrain of self-discovery and the sexual liberation that might come from daring to channel your intrinsic courage instead of relying on liquid courage. The best views don't need rosé-colored glasses.

Checking In

How did alcohol show up in your previous relationships?

How do you want your relationship communication style to evolve as you drink less or not at all?

How did/does alcohol impact your communication skills? Do you feel more comfortable discussing unpleasant topics after a few drinks? If so, why?

Reflect on a recent ex. Who were you before the relationship began? How did this relationship impact that version of you? Who are you now that it's over?

What role did alcohol play in your past fights or breakups?

How do you feel about liquid courage now, after reading this book?

What does living an authentically courageous life look like to you?

What role does alcohol play in your future love life?

RESOURCES

Organizations

Big Vision An organization supporting young adults (ages 18–30) who are struggling with substance use. *www.bigvision.nyc*

Movendi An international NGO advocating for sobriety on a personal and community level. *www.movendi.ngo*

Sans Bar An Austin-based nonalcoholic bar offering virtual events where you can learn how to make mocktails or start your own nonalcoholic drink business, created by Chris Marshall. *www.thesansbar.com*

Sober Black Girls Club A community offering resources and virtual meetups for Black women interested in sobriety, created by Khadi A. Oluwatoyin. *www.soberblackgirlsclub.com*

Sober Mom Squad A community for moms exploring alcohol-free life that offers meetups and webinars, created by Emily Lynn Paulson. *www .sobermomsquad.com*

Blogs

Sober Curator One-stop shop for the latest and greatest news in the sober world, created by Alysse Bryson. *www.thesobercurator.com*

SobrieTea Party The blog I started in 2015 documenting my sobriety since day one. *www.sobrieteaparty.com*

Zero Proof Nation The go-to spot for information about nonalcoholic beverages and bars, created by Laura Silverman. *www.zeroproof nation.com*

Podcasts

F*cking Sober A serialized account of one woman's first ninety days sober, hosted by Katie Mack. *www.fckingsoberpodcast.com*

Recovery Rocks My podcast about getting sober but staying cool, hosted by Tawny Lara and Lisa Smith. *www.tawnylara.com/podcast*

Sober Black Girls Club The podcast arm of Sober Black Girls Club, hosted by Khadi A. Oluwatoyin and J. Nicole Jones. *podcasts.apple.com/us /podcast/sober-black-girls-club/id1609305414*

Sober Curious Conversations about guests' various relationships with substances and sobriety, hosted by Ruby Warrington. *podcasts.apple .com/us/podcast/sober-curious/id1460377009*

A Sober Girls Guide Sobriety and mental health discussion with a sobriety life coach, hosted by Jessica Jeboult. *www.asobergirlsguide.com /podcast*

The Sober Gay A podcast about sobriety in the queer community, hosted by Dillan Gay. *www.thesobergay.com*

Books

Drinking Games: A Memoir by Sarah Levy

Girl Walks Out of a Bar: A Memoir by Lisa Smith

Good Drinks: Alcohol-Free Recipes for When You're Not Drinking for Whatever Reason by Julia Bainbridge

Highlight Real: Finding Honesty & Recovery Beyond the Filtered Life by Emily Lynn Paulson

It's Not About the Wine: The Loaded Truth Behind Mommy Wine Culture by Celeste Yvonne

Not Drinking Tonight: A Guide to Creating a Sober Life You Love by Amanda E. White

Overcome: A Memoir of Abuse, Addiction, Sex Work, and Recovery by Amber van de Bunt

A Piece of Cake: A Memoir by Cupcake Brown

Push Off from Here: 9 Essential Truths to Get You Through Life (and Everything Else) by Laura McKowen

Quit Like a Woman: The Radical Choice to Not Drink in a Culture Obsessed with Alcohol by Holly Whitaker

Sex in Recovery: A Meeting Between the Covers by Jennifer Matesa

Sober Curious: The Blissful Sleep, Greater Focus, Limitless Presence, and Deep Connection Awaiting Us All on the Other Side of Alcohol by Ruby Warrington

Sober Curious Reset: Change the Way You Drink in 100 Days or Less by Ruby Warrington

Stash: My Life in Hiding by Laura Cathcart Robbins

This Naked Mind: Control Alcohol, Find Freedom, Discover Happiness & Change Your Life by Annie Grace

Unbottled Potential: Break Up with Alcohol and Break Through to Your Best Life by Amanda Kuda

We Are the Luckiest: The Surprising Magic of Sober Life by Laura McKowen

SELECTED BIBLIOGRAPHY

For a complete list of references consulted,
visit quirkbooks.com/dryhumping.

Chapter 1

Kelly, Megan, Rachel Simmons, Shihwe Wang, Shane Kraus, Joseph Dona-
hue, and Katharine A. Phillips. "Motives to Drink Alcohol Among Individu-
als with Body Dysmorphic Disorder." *Journal of Obsessive-Compulsive
and Related Disorders* 12 (January 2017): 52–57. https://www.science
direct.com/science/article/abs/pii/S2211364916301270.

Chapter 3

"Hinge's Summer 2022 Dating Predictions: Gen Z Daters Are Rejecting
Drinking on Dates." Hinge (website), June 15, 2022. https://www.hinge.co
/press/summer-2022-dating-predictions.

Chapter 4

Duncan, Tracey Anne. "Getting Sober Hits Different for Queer People." *Mic*,
May 16, 2022. https://www.mic.com/identity/queer-people
-sobriety-journey.

Santilli, Mara. "What Is Emotional Sobriety? Here's How to Practice This
Self-Growth Tool." *Women's Health*, October 3, 2021. https://www.
womenshealthmag.com/health/a37825555/what-is-emotional
-sobriety-heres-how-to-practice-this-self-growth-tool.

Chapter 6

Schrieks, Ilse, Annette Stafleu, Victor L. Kallen, Marc Grootjen, Renger F.
Witkamp, and Henk F. J. Hendriks. "The Biphasic Effects of Moderate

Alcohol Consumption with a Meal on Ambiance-Induced Mood and Autonomic Nervous System Balance: A Randomized Crossover Trial." *PLOS ONE* (January 21, 2014). https://journals.plos.org/plosone/article?id=10.1371/journal.pone.0086199.

Chapter 7

Engle, Gigi. "What Are Emotional Aphrodisiacs, and How Can They Help Your Sex Life?" *InsideHook*, May 24, 2022. https://www.insidehook.com/article/sex-and-dating/emotional-aphrodisiacs-help-sex-life.

Gallagher, Kimberly. *Aphrodisiac: The Herbal Path to Healthy Sexual Fulfillment and Vital Living.* Carlsbad, CA: Hay House Inc., 2021.

Wolfe, Rachel. "The Latest Innovation in Beer Is Water in a Can." *Wall Street Journal,* August 19, 2022. https://www.wsj.com/articles/the-latest-innovation-in-beer-is-water-in-a-can-11660916880.

Chapter 8

Barbour, Anadel Baughn. *Sex in Sobriety: A Qualitative Narrative Exploration of the Utilization of Mindfulness Practices for Enjoyable Sober Sex.* Pittsburgh, PA: Dorrance Publishing, 2017.

McCabe, Sean E., Tonda L. Hughes, Brady T. West, Phil Veliz, and Carol J. Boyd. "DSM-5 Alcohol Use Disorder Severity as a Function of Sexual Orientation Discrimination: A National Study." *Alcoholism, Clinical and Experimental Research* 43, no. 3 (March 2019): 497–508. https://doi.org/10.1111/acer.13960.

Chapter 13

George, William H., Kelly Cue Davis, Julia R. Heiman, Jeanette Norris, Susan A. Stoner, Rebecca L. Schacht, Christian S. Hendershot, and Kelly F. Kajumulo. "Women's Sexual Arousal: Effects of High Alcohol Dosages and

Self-Control Instructions." *Hormones and Behavior* 59, no. 5 (May 2011): 730–738. https://doi.org/10.1016/j.yhbeh.2011.03.006.

Lara, Tawny. "The True Cost of Drinking Is Much Higher Than You Think." *The Temper,* January 10, 2019. https://www.thetemper.com/cost-of-drinking.

Van Lawick van Pabst, Albertine E., Lydia E. Devenney, and Joris C. Verster. "Sex Differences in the Presence and Severity of Alcohol Hangover Symptoms." *Journal of Clinical Medicine* 8, no. 6 (2019): 867. https://www.ncbi.nlm.nih.gov/pmc/articles/PMC6617014.

ACKNOWLEDGMENTS

This book would not exist without Ruth Danon teaching me to "let yourself write bad." Ruth's approach to writing showed me that it's necessary to get words on the page, regardless of how "good" they are. I spent years self-editing in my head before daring to bring those ideas to fruition.

To my agent, Eric Smith, thanks for being as excited about this book as I am, for putting up with my annoying dry humping puns, and for tolerating my Capricorn anxiety.

To my editor, Jess Zimmerman, you elevated my vision for this book. Collaborating with you teaches me about myself, which ultimately teaches me more about my writing. You made this book more accessible and approachable. Thanks for helping me become a better writer.

To my publisher, Quirk, thanks for taking a chance on a niche book about a not-so-niche intersection. This is the book I needed when I was newly sober and terrified of dating, let alone having sex, without alcohol.

To Sarah Wolford and Anne Porter, my kick-ass SobrieTeam, who handle the minutiae so I can focus on writing.

To my beta readers and dear friends, Lisa Smith, Emma Poole, Tracey Stubbs, and Katie Mack: thanks for reading (and rereading) this manuscript. Your ojos on this book helped me more than you know.

To my book proposal coach turned bestie, Irina Gonzalez, you held me accountable for getting words on the page and then editing those words to make sense.

To Gabrielle Kassel, Morgan Mandriota, and our sex writer group chat, having a safe space to discuss the madness of our industry keeps me (relatively) sane.

To Lisa Smith, my podcast cohost and bestie, thanks for taking me under your wing because you knew I had a story to tell. I'm forever addicted to your shindig.

To Ruby Warrington, thanks for calling me the Sober Sexpert and patiently letting me talk out my myriad book ideas until I got to the right one. Creating the term *sober curious* truly changed the world. You came up with a term that helps people evaluate their relationship with alcohol without having to identify as alcoholics or addicts. I'm honored to be in your numinous orbit.

To Holly Whitaker, you're busy AF, yet you always make time to help up-and-coming authors. Thanks for writing *Quit Like a Woman* and quite literally changing the world.

To Gene and Jack at Road Recovery, thank you for creating an inclusive, nuanced program that helped me work through my shit while learning the importance of being of service. Combining music and creativity with peer support is truly genius! Y'all are changing countless lives. I know you've made Jeff proud!

To my therapist, Lynn, for helping me make sense of my past so I can live a happier today and build a solid future. I now have the tools to live (read: THRIVE) without alcohol!

Mom, thanks for teaching me that my voice is worth hearing. You saved all of my articles (and hate mail!) from when I wrote for the *Waco Tribune-Herald* at age 14. I look at that scrapbook regularly, in awe of the teenager who had the audacity to write about normalizing gay marriage, advocating for realistic sex ed, and legalizing weed while growing up in a conservative town. Oh, and thanks for keeping me stocked in HEB tortillas and jerky during the writing process.

Dad, thanks for teaching me how to rock since day one. Watching you chase your dreams gave me the courage to chase my own. You gotta believe!

To Tracey Stubbs, my aunt/beta reader/financial advisor/reading buddy, thanks for femme-splaining Gpa-isms that help me become a more responsible person.

To Nick, my Sour Humanoid. You fermented my heart. You saw this book evolve so much over the years and encouraged me to keep going when I didn't think I could. I'm grateful to have lots of sober sex with you.

To my sweet fur babies who went through hell while I wrote this book. Clara, you're still nose-dipping the snow in my dreams. Meg White, you're the cutest cyclops meow.

To Waco, Texas, thanks for my first byline (Waco Trib!), the countless shenanigans, and for naming tacos after me.

To Washington Heights, thanks for being such a beautiful community. I wrote most of this book at Uptown Garrison, sweated it out at Studio in the Heights, practiced yoga with Emma, perused the shelves at Word Up books for inspiration, and kept fresh bouquets from Anthony Flowers on my desk.

A mis ancestros mexicanos y judíos que nunca tuvieron el privilegio de aprender a leer y mucho menos a escribir.

To the generations of women and nonbinary folks who weren't allowed to express themselves sexually, I see you. I write for you.

To Sigur Rós, Khruangbin, and the *Stranger Things* score: thanks for keeping my brain stimulated and focused while writing and researching.

Thanks to everyone else who sent me encouraging texts, emails, flowers, and gift cards while writing this book.

To younger me, you never needed liquid courage, girl! You had intrinsic courage all along. Thanks for staying alive through some really tough times so we could write this book together.

To you, dear reader. Thanks for dry humping with me. Remember that liquid courage is a BS marketing tactic. You don't need it to have a good time on dates, between the sheets, or in a relationship.